A TRAGIC AFFAIR

It was love at first sight between Onesimus and the beautiful slave Aurelia. But she was only fifteen and her fate had been sealed by her master: she would be a Roman courtesan, forever beyond the reach—and dreams—of a mere servant.

Years would pass before they met again, and much would happen to transform Onesimus from obedient slave into a rebellious fugitive thief. The unrest began when his master Philemon turned away from old gods and toward the new religion, Christianity, becoming a weak man in the disillusioned eyes of Onesimus.

That was when he decided to escape. Stealing Philemon's jewels to finance his trip to Rome, he set out to carve a free life for himself, and to liberate Aurelia from her new home, the infamous court of Nero.

Then he met Paul, the man who changed his life....

Paul and Mary Alciere
62 Downer Avenue
Hingham, MA 02043-1103

LETTER TO PHILEMON

WINTHROP and FRANCES NEILSON

FAMILY LIBRARY   E   NEW YORK

LETTER TO PHILEMON

A FAMILY LIBRARY BOOK

Second printing May, 1974

ISBN 0-515-03216-6

Copyright © 1962 by Winthrop and Frances Neilson
All Rights Reserved

Printed in the United States of America

FAMILY LIBRARY is published by Pyramid Publications
919 Third Avenue, New York, New York 10022, U.S.A.

With gratitude for his sincerity,
for his vision, and for his resolute life,
we dedicate this book to our friend,
EDUARDO ANDRADE

AUTHORS' NOTE

The shortest Book in the New Testament scarcely fills one page. It is the personal letter which St. Paul wrote to a man named Philemon, who lived at Colossae in Phrygia in Asia Minor. In it Paul asks his friend Philemon, a Christian, to take back and treat kindly his runaway slave, Onesimus. As a letter, it is perhaps one of the most beautiful and moving ever written.

The facts in the letter itself, and related facts which traditional records verify, reveal that the story of the runaway slave must have been a poignant example of a man's discovery of faith. Exactly how Onesimus fled from Colossae, later met Paul, and came to be converted by the Apostle can only be surmised. Nothing outside the letter is known definitely about Onesimus, or of Philemon and his family—Apphia, his wife, and Archippus, his son. One report states that they were all eventually martyred, but there is no proof. A Christian bishop named Onesimus is mentioned in the records fifty years later, but there is no reason to assume he was the same man.

It is not absolutely certain where Paul was at the time he wrote the letter, which coincided in time with the Epistle, he wrote to the Colossians. Nevertheless, authorities do generally believe that he was in Rome, and that he was imprisoned in his own house. These scholars all agree that Paul himself wrote the letter.

Our story of Onesimus is a novel of a search for faith. We have used the facts and the interpretations from the records insofar as they exist. For example:

The riot in Ephesus is described in The Acts of the Apostles. There was a violent storm in the harbor of Ostia in the year 62 A.D. which destroyed two hundred ships. Research is clear on how the worship of Mithra flourished in Asia Minor and spread to Rome. There has been no necessity to surmise on historical facts.

We have had to take very few liberties with the actual chronology of events. There is little known about specific dates of that time, but we feel that our time sequence is reasonable.

Readers may wish to know which among our principal characters are real and which fictitious. We have created Aurelia, although the facts of Octavia's slave girls are true. Persilio is fictitious. So are Dario and Yrujo the Spaniard among lesser characters. All of the other major characters are authentic. Paul's physical characteristics appear in only one ancient source, perhaps not reliable. The description we have used is fitting, however, to this tremendous personality.

A story should develop of itself, through reading and association. Ours grew in Rome as we stood among ruins of Mithraic temples, as we walked the Appian Way and passed along the ancient streets, and murmured a prayer in the dank, unwholesome Mamertine Prison which still preserves its fearful memories.

And, by the strangest coincidence, we discovered that our small apartment in Rome—in the Palazzo Doria on the Via Lata and the Corso where we wrote much of this book—was built over the remains of St. Paul's house. The caretaker of the church, part of the Palazzo Doria, on the corner of the Corso will show any visitor the foundations of this house down under the modern city.

WINTHROP AND FRANCES NEILSON

LETTER TO PHILEMON

I

I am Onesimus. Greetings, and also from Aurelia, my so dearly beloved, who shares with me the secrets of faith so long hidden from us.

Aboard this ship, with its great sail set to the fair wind, I will set down the full account of our struggles to escape from slavery . . . indeed, from those two kinds of slavery which so often enchain the human soul. Aurelia and I were slaves to our masters, and the bonds have been cut away. We were slaves in our hearts also, and the fetters likewise have been forced apart. These things are miracles, wrought by faith.

The shores of Italy recede across the sea. The crushing substance of Rome diminishes with the distance. God willing, Athens lies ahead. Aurelia, my beautiful and beloved, sits by my side while the soothing sun heals the scars of those searing lashes across her injured body. I start my manuscript at the beginning, the very beginning, before all these things came upon our way.

Of my own origin I know nothing, except that I was one of a group of slaves purchased in the market at Antioch when I was about the age of six. I do remember the great cage or pen where, under the dazzling white heat of the piazza, men moved back and forth inspecting the nearly naked humans for sale. I remember my childish anger at the fingers which poked me and lifted my brief chlamys so that the purchasers could see if I were Hebrew circumcised.

I have forgotten the long journey through Asia Minor to the house of Philemon in Colossae, ancient city of

Phrygia on the banks of the river Lycus. I remember that at first the immense villa with its formality and strict discipline frightened me. The women of the slaves' quarters where I was placed said that I was rebellious and stupid. They boxed my ears and wasted little sympathy on me. I am sure that I had good cause for my loathing of those women.

My master Philemon, as head of a great household and widespread business, had little to do with most of the slaves. His steward Zalgrebbo and his older son Archippus took care of domestic affairs. I have come to know Philemon now as a man of kindness and justice, one whom age and faith have tempered. But as a small boy I used to see him from far off striding through the halls, a huge man of broad shoulders and the blackest of black beards. The dark of his eyes matched his beard, and flashed with sparks that could turn instantly to angry lightning. He was an exacting man, fair in his dealings but terrible in his rages. Sorry was the fate of any slave who risked his temper.

Yet toward his family Philemon was gentle and yielding. This was especially true of Persilio, his younger son, the family favorite. Persilio was of the same age as I. We were allowed to play together, and we became as close friends as the heavy-browed pedagogue in charge of the master's son would permit. Persilio was delicate and pale, a solemn young boy who was much like his mother Apphia. He was always dressed in silken chlamys with borders of gold braid. He had golden sandals, and perfume behind his neck. Yet it never seemed strange to me that my own shirt by comparison was of gray cotton and my sandals of unfinished leather. I was not the son of the master.

Apphia was the one whom I came to love with a youthful adoration that amounted to worship. Unchanged by the years, Philemon's wife is still among the most beautiful of women. Her heavily braided hair has the dark russet color of embers in an ebbing fire, seeming to be ready at any moment to burst into flame. Her eyes twinkle sympathetically, and her mouth is quick with her own beguiling smile. She is fragile as the shell of a bird's egg in its nest. And Apphia has the heavenly quality of charm and vivacity. To a small boy she could well be a goddess come to earth. To men she is woman turned goddess.

Her dressing hour in late afternoon was the time Apphia entertained her son Persilio. His pedagogue would leave him at her apartment, and the mother and boy would talk all the while the slave girls performed their duties upon her. Finally one day I was allowed to come with Persilio after play. I was awed, and sat silently at one side of the room. Apphia awakened in me a yearning for something I had not known. She contained a mother's comforts which I had never experienced. I longed for the caress she gave to unmindful Persilio.

"You stay so quietly," Apphia said one day. "A boy must not be so quiet; a boy should be laughing and mischievous. You are more quiet than Persilio, and Persilio is also too quiet."

"He does not play so quietly," Persilio said. He looked at me and I squirmed all over with shyness.

"They say in the servants' hall," one of the slave girls told her mistress, "that he is stupid."

"No, he does not look stupid," Apphia said. "He has a good forehead, and good eyes. See, how his chin is already forming a stubborn thrust. He will never be stupid."

All the girls stared at me now, with little giggles. I knew I had become very red in the face. I opened my mouth and closed it again. Apphia took pity on me for my misery. She leaped from her couch and came to me.

"You are being teased," she cried. "It is not fair!"

She encircled me with her arms, and I was lost in the masses of loose hair which fell around me. I felt the pressure of her cheek against mine. I trembled in the ecstasy of her embrace, as I would have in the arms of a mother of my own.

"Now," she said, "you know that you belong in Philemon's household. I think that you have been treated as one outside our walls, unfortunate child."

Each day after that, Apphia never failed in her caress for me—although not as warm as her attentions to Persilio. I became very happy, and looked forward with joyful heart to the afternoon hour of being with Persilio's mother. I found that I could laugh and enter the lighthearted conversation. The girls attending Apphia carried reports of me back to the quarters where I stayed, and gradually it came to be understood that I was Persilio's playmate and should be treated with consideration. I gained in confidence within myself and began to realize that even for a slave life was an object of personal importance.

One day an event occurred which changed my daily world and charted my future. We were in Apphia's room as usual when all at once Philemon came to the door. Everyone was startled except Philemon himself, who laughed with great amusement. The girls hastily put from sight the jars of pomade and pots of color which contained the mysteries of beauty known only to women. I rose to my feet and bowed, as Persilio did also in respect of his father.

"Oh, you invade my sanctuary!" Apphia cried, pretending great anger. "No man must ever enter a woman's presence at this time of day. You are a thief, stealing privacy."

"By a husband's prerogative," Philemon replied, his dark eyes alight. "A husband, after all, cannot steal what is already his own."

"No, no," she said, and laughed at him. "A woman always keeps something of her own, something that no husband can ever have. Learn that, my much-loved Philemon. Even my girls can tell you so."

She ran to him with hair loose, and he clasped her in his arms. Between Apphia and Philemon, as I know it now, there has never been anything but love, trust and respect. It took me long years to learn what these things mean between husband and wife. I know them now, with Aurelia my beloved, but in the years of youth one cannot understand.

Then he released her and pretended anger himself.

"See, though, how your own words fly back at you!" he roared. "You have males in your presence, watchful, curious males to whom you are giving out the deepest secrets of women. Where is your shame before these incipient men, no less than two of them at that?"

He pointed to Persilio, and then at me. I trembled, not knowing how much of this was serious.

"A baby can suck his mother's breast," Apphia replied.

Philemon glanced at her. "Hmm. I think the greatest of women's secrets is to know how to say the last, unquenchable word. All right—I have left Archippus outside the door. As long as these two babes are here, may I bring in the one only slightly older?"

"But of course," Apphia said. "That you should leave my son outside my door! Archippus—" She went to the entrance and called. "Come in, Archippus, and never pay such attention to your father."

Archippus entered. He was much like Philemon although slighter, and slower, and less certain of what to do. He was nearly grown to manhood himself, and he already shared in much of his father's business affairs.

"So, Archippus, we are welcome after all in the sanctum of women," Philemon said.

"I would not wish to intrude," Archippus said stiffly.

"Nonsense!" Apphia cried. "You are my son. Are

not my sons welcome always? And my husband?" she added.

She laughed with the good nature which Apphia has always possessed. But the serving maids, dressed in their short work tunics, had already shrunk back at Archippus' entrance. I had heard it whispered that Archippus often took the younger slave girls into his room at night.

Philemon looked at me. He said, "Then who is this one, who is not family? Is he to be as one of our own, in our intimate quarters?"

Apphia said quickly, "I have asked him here. He is Persilio's playmate. He is a child who knows nothing."

The master was staring at me. "Persilio's playmate?"

"Father, he is one of those we obtained from Antioch," Archippus explained. "You will remember. He cost us nothing additional, and we hoped he might grow up to be useful."

Philemon walked slowly to where I was standing trembling. To my surprise, he dropped down to one knee before me, so that his head was more nearly on a level with mine. He looked at me closely, examining the long narrowness of my face, the blueness of my eyes, and my curly blond hair. I do not know whether I was a promising child, but he appeared to be satisfied. He touched my chin and felt the muscles of my shoulders and ribs.

"I remember the boy," he said at last. "So we are hoping you may grow up to be useful to us? You seem to show the promise of it." Then he continued, "Have you been given a name yet? No matter. From now you are to be called Onesimus. That word means 'useful.' Have you heard it before?"

I had not, of course. The master spoke kindly now, but I was too fascinated by his black eyes, burning like coals. I could not look away from them.

Apphia came up to touch the master's shoulder. "I

am glad," she said. "We can teach this boy many things. He could study with Persilio."

Philemon nodded. "You are obedient? You do all that you are told?" he asked me.

"I am good so that I will not be whipped," I answered with the best voice I could.

He smiled a little. "We hope that you will never have to be whipped," he said. "We must expect more of you than the necessity of whipping. You may begin your studies with Persilio at once. In time you will learn to write and to read, to be proficient in the Latin and the Hebrew languages as well as Greek. You must learn numbers and how to count. There is a world of knowledge for you to gain so that you may indeed be Onesimus—useful—to us in our business."

"Yes," I replied because I thought he expected me to say it, not because I understood fully.

Philemon rose to his feet, and turned to his older son. "Archippus," he said, "I will trust to you that my orders for this boy are carried out."

Archippus, like everyone else in the room, had been looking at me all the while. I doubted that he approved of his father's decision, but he said nothing. Persilio gazed at me solemnly, and then he suddenly smiled. I was glad.

And Apphia patted my head for reassurance. Then I was truly happy.

I entered at once on my studies with Persilio. We were taken each morning to the house of the teacher Demetris, three streets away from Philemon's villa. Persilio's pedagogue escorted us. This man-nurse was gruff and blunt, and slow to accept my presence in Persilio's company. Perhaps he resented my status as privileged.

I enjoyed the early walk through the streets of Colossae. I saw the donkeys carrying water jugs, the ox-carts with vegetables, soldiers from Rome, magistrates on horseback, the camels from beyond Palmyra. I liked to see the foodshops, the cheese and fruit stores where women bargained for prices. I enjoyed the warm, acrid smells of the streets as we passed among the crowds of people while the pedagogue made sure the son of Philemon came to no harm. I was supposed to walk a step behind Persilio. If I forgot, the pedagogue would pull my hair to make me remember my position.

Our lessons were of the first letters of the alphabet, first words of languages, and easy numbers for counting. Although Persilio had started learning before me, I seemed to catch up with him quickly. We had fun with the teacher Demetris. We told him he had fleas in his enormous beard.

I came to know well the rest of Philemon's household —almost all slaves like myself. Zalgrebbo, the steward, himself a slave, maintained the discipline of iron which pervaded the villa. Whenever a slave was whipped or tortured for infraction of rules, at Zalgrebbo's order the rest of us were brought in to watch. Like the others, I learned at last to remain unmoved while a man's bones were cracked on the rack, or scarcely to pale at the sight of a woman hanging by the wrists while the flogging whip scorched her back and buttocks. Sounds of screaming pain fall heedlessly on ears soon deafened by experience. Blood and death were almost as commonplace then as they are now. In fact, I became quite scornful of any who broke too quickly under the force of torture.

The clerk Spyridus, a silent, grizzled man, was the one to check inventories of materials in Philemon's warehouses. Our master was a trader, dealing mostly in Laodicean wool, the fine black wool for which Colossae and neighboring Laodicea are famous. Philemon exported the local wool, as well as jewels and the new fine silks from the East, to all parts of the Roman Empire. Camel trains came in from India and the far corners of

Arabia, and lines of four-wheeled wagons moved west to Ephesus, the coastal port for the Mediterranean. Our master was a shrewd merchant, as attested by his constantly increasing riches. The clerk Spyridus spent long days and nights counting the materials coming and going, and though a slave like the rest of us, he was privileged, even being above reproof by the all-powerful Zalgrebbo.

Whenever I could escape from the women in charge of me, I would go to the warehouses and watch while Sypridus slowly transferred rubies, emeralds, and onyx from one box to another, or superintended slaves sorting out rolls of cloth from the Orient or iron tools from Rome. The merchandise held a great fascination for me, not only of curiosity. I touched the silks which felt good in my fingers, and held pearls in my hands to watch their changing lights. I found myself longing to possess for my own these treasures of glowing colors and rich textures. Yet I never dared to keep anything, easy as it would have been, or even to ask Spyridus for bits of samples. I was afraid of the whip that would of a certainty have been decreed for me.

Slowly, as I grew older, my position in the villa household came to be firmly fixed. As always happens to slaves who are permanently owned by one master, my absolute loyalty to the family of Philemon was demanded. At that time of my youth it was fully given by me.

I could not have dreamed that rebellion would one day enter my heart.

II

When we came to an age of understanding, Persilio and I were taken regularly to learn the principles of religion at the grotto of Mithra.

My master and his family worshipped Mithra, the all-powerful God of Light, who with his ally the Sun God ruled the world and heaven for eternal time. According to belief, Mithra led the forces of righteousness against the underworld powers of evil in the great struggle for men's souls. This faith in Mithra, stepped in mysticism, came from ancient Oriental and Persian origins. It had only reached westward to Colossae in recent times.

Philemon was a man of deep devotion and sincerity. He found in the worship of Mithra a spiritual strength which the old gods of Athens and Rome never possessed for him. Throughout Asia Minor men were seeking after beliefs of deeper significance than western creeds, and the search had given rise to acceptance of Oriental faiths including Mithraism. The deities of ancient Greece, with their hoary histories of incest and murder, rape and seduction, lost favor against a mystical religion such as Mithra's which offered salvation from evil and promised immortality after death.

These things I came to know later. To the imagination of a boy, Mithra was more a hero than a divinity. He was considered a young man of great strength, and he waged ceaseless war against the evil spirits which he himself had cast out from heaven. According to legend, Mithra in the beginning had sprung full-grown from a rock, a dagger in one hand and a torch in the other.

Shepherds in the fields had witnessed with awe the miracle of his origin, and they had brought to him offerings of their best possessions.

The legends of Mithra were sculptured on panels of stone kept in the grottoes of worship. Persilio and I heard with wonder the stories told, and we often gazed fearfully at the carvings. One legend described how the god had shot an arrow into a rock, from which burst forth an everlasting fountain of water for thirsting humans. A panel pictured Mithra sitting under a fig tree, naked except for the conical Phrygian cap he always wore, sheltering himself from the wind while he made clothes of fig leaves. Another showed the beginning of his partnership with the Sun God, also known as a young man, who was pictured kneeling in supplication before the great God of Light. Mithra had touched the God of the Sun with a holy emblem and placed a radiant crown upon his head. Afterward the two gods sat together on a couch before a dining table spread with holy bread, and together they drank from a sacred cup.

The most important legend of all, and the one on which the faith itself was founded, concerned the titanic struggle of Mithra and the great symbolic bull. The god challenged the bull, and a fearful battle followed. The series of carvings showed Mithra lifting the animal from the ground, and then the god being tossed high on angry horns. At length Mithra carried the bull into a cave, and there he slew it by plunging his dagger deep into its throat. This last scene, the most revered of all the stories, represented the god kneeling over the dying beast with weapon poised while symbolic animals of evil, the scorpion and the serpent, tore the bull's genitals, and a dog drank its blood. Yet from the ground around sprang plants and flowers, testifying to new life always growing up from death. So Mithra destroyed, in the form of the bull, those passions of the flesh which bound the spiritual force of the soul.

My first experience in the worship of Mithra left me terrified and yet exhilarated almost to obsession. Persilio had been to the temple once before, and he tried to describe in advance the great light, the music of the litanies, and the cleansing of the body and the spirit by blood. The reality far surpassed his power of telling. Mithraic chapels from ancient times have been built into caves or grottoes suggestive of the cave where the god slew the bull. The temple at Colossae, like most others, was small in size and designed simply. Beyond the open portico at the entrance there was a chapel, and beyond this a room called the *appartatorium,* the room of the priests or robing place. From there stairs led down into the crypt, the sanctuary itself, which held the altar with its sacred fire endlessly burning. Attending the altar fire, representing the burning light of the stars, were two virgins shrouded in white.

I was cold with fright on my first walk down those stairs. The red-robed priest led the way, and I remember still the solemn, shuffling footsteps of the congregation descending. The crypt was bright with torchlight and heavy with smoke which filled one's nose. Stone benches lined the side walls for the use of the initiated. The uninitiated like myself stood at the back. A choir chanted endlessly while the motionless virgins kneeled in prayer. The priest approached the altar to prepare a sacrifice.

The ceremony was breathtaking in grandeur and solemnity. I felt near to fainting with emotion. I clutched at Persilio's hand, and noticed Apphia smiling with encouragement from her place on the side bench. Then the priest joined the litany, the chant rose higher, and the virgins rose to fan the fire into flame. A great exaltation filled all the congregation and arms and faces lifted to receive the blessing of the source of life. I remember my feelings soaring until I was aware of no place or time but only of unbounded realms of space forever. The priest sprinkled drops of fresh bull's blood over the fire to signify the cleansing of the spirit, and the initiated drank the juice of the sacred vine from the holy cup.

At the end of the service, sweat had come upon my brow, not alone from the heat of the crypt. I saw, too, the paleness of Persilio's face. He had been as much affected as I was myself.

The high sense of the glory of Mithra grew with me through many times of worship. The god became as close to me as he was to all of Philemon's family.

Not all of the household of the villa were believers in Mithra. Many of the slave servants, especially older ones, followed other gods. Philemon never forced his people into a religious belief. Like most masters, he held that the physical self could be owned, but never the spiritual. Bodies belonged to men, souls to the gods.

Persilio and I discussed these things together. Often we would go to the villa garden overlooking the river Lycus and its deep dark gorge below the town. A stone bench was placed under the green of palms and the delicacy of mimosa. Here we talked with the seriousness of youth, discovering every day new facets of thought.

"Yesterday I saw a man die," Persilio said once. "He was seized on the street by the spirit of death, and he lay on the ground and died while we watched."

"What did you do?" I asked.

"Nothing. What can one do in the face of death? The man ceased to be. Before sleeping last night I thought of it for a long time."

"A man does not cease to be," I said. "We are taught that men have souls. If his soul be received kindly by the gods, he will continue to live in heaven."

"That is the promise by Mithra," Persilio said. "But I did not recognize this man. I do not think he is one of those who worship with us in the grotto."

"Does that condemn his soul?" I wondered.

Persilio was silent, and then he said, "I told my brother Archippus that I would like to be a priest of Mithra."

"You!" I exclaimed. "And what did he say?"

"He was angry, because, he said, a son of Philemon is not born to be a priest. We are to be masters, not slaves."

When I looked at Persilio, I saw that his thin, pale face was troubled. So Archippus thought that the lot of a priest was equal to slavery! I, a slave, meditated on this in my mind.

"To be born as you are," I said enviously to Persilio, "is to be born into a state of heaven on earth. Archippus is quite right."

In our talks one would not have thought of Persilio and me as master and slave. Yet, with time, that inescapable fact began more and more to grow between us. We realized without saying it to each other that our closeness of friendship must dissolve under the cold light of becoming older. We became more aware of it when Persilio's interests began to be diverted from mine. He turned to the study of music; I was placed with the clerk Spyridus to learn the work of the warehouses.

At the approach of adolescence I was no longer allowed access to Apphia's private apartment. It was an inevitable result of puberty. Nevertheless, I was deeply disappointed, especially as Persilio was still allowed to go to his mother's room. The mistress remained most kind to me, but the caresses stopped. Then my loneliness grew to melancholy, and I was seized with the youthful affliction of feeling life's injustice.

Yet I knew that I was growing taller, broader in the shoulders, more full of body. When I looked at the young slave maidens I felt the spring in me. They would not look back in my direction. They laughed and called me still too young.

Persilio, on the other hand, concerned himself little with girls. He who could have ordered them to come to him would not avail himself. He grew tall as I did, but he did not become strong. His arms were weak, his chest hollow. One might have inferred that some lingering indisposition beset him.

It must have been at about this time of life that rebellion entered my heart. I can guess now that I was angry at Persilio, my friend, who after all was not friend but master. If this indeed was one cause of my later misdeeds, then I was guilty of miscarriage of loyalty. For Persilio never gave me cause for a servile feeling. I created the trouble in my own mind. It was a difficult time for me, for I had lost Apphia's tenderness and was about to lose Persilio's companionship. It was not easy for me to accept my lot gently.

Spyridus the clerk seemed to know what I was thinking. He would stop in his work and say to me, "One is what one is born to be. Let no man step across his line of destiny, lest his feet stray into the darkness of disaster." The words rang fair, but I laughed at the old man.

"Some day the gods will unfold the world to me," I boasted. "I pray to Mithra for freedom in time to come. Then I too like Philemon can be a citizen, and have such wealth as this!" I flung at Spyridus a section of precious silk from beyond the lands of the Indies. "I am Onesimus, the useful one. To whom should I be more useful than to myself?"

"Spoken as by a fool," Spyridus muttered. "If Zalgrebbo hears such words he will skin you on his whipping post."

"Zalgrebbo!" I cried. "What care I for him? I am Persilio's friend. And Apphia would intercede for me."

Foolish words on my part. "You will learn," Spyridus said cryptically. He went back to his work.

Shortly afterward a new boy named Dario entered the household. He was purchased to work as a stable boy for Philemon's horses and the camels of visiting traders. He was older than I, and I never really came to like him. His character was coarse and loose and his language rough. Yet, as can happen between the older and the younger, Dario overpowered me with his leadership, and in my new aloneness, more and more bereft of Persilio, I fell in with the stable boy as companion.

I tell this miserable story concerning Dario as it became an event in the progress of my life. I would rather leave it untold.

In Philemon's service we were permitted a certain amount of liberty to go into the town or to visit neighboring villas, so long as we performed our work and gave the strictest obedience to rules. Dario became friendly with a group of boys in the town, and sometimes he took me with him when they met at one of the wineshops. Yet they were older, and during their conversations I felt sharply the difference in years. I had not the experience to understand what they said, especially when their talk concerned women.

That I might offer something of my own in turn, I took Dario to the temple of Mithra. He went with me a number of times. We would stand side by side at the back of the crypt during the rites of worship. I was pleased and believed I had brought a convert to the God of Light.

He laughed when I spoke of this. "I care for one god as well as another," he said. "They are the same to me, if gods exist at all. I go to the grotto with you to look at the maidens of the altar."

I was much disturbed by this irreverent disclosure. It was my first experience with cynicism about religion. The words of Dario became the more distressing because secretly I myself had gazed at the virgins with thoughts far from holy respect. Now I felt that my own sin was uncovered, at least in my conscience.

The virgins who attended the altar fire served voluntarily for certain periods of time, usually not long, but during which they had to fulfill the strictest vows of chastity and purity. The girls were selected for youth and beauty, so as to be most pleasing to the god. The maidens of Colossae felt themselves especially honored to be selected for Mithra's service, despite long hours of physical hardship spent on their knees in prayer. Usually they served in pairs, and always they were shrouded in white robes from head to feet.

It ought to be explained that in the precincts of Mithra's temples no distinction exists of class or worldly status. A slave, a freedman, and the master of a great villa are alike in Mithra's sight. The soul is above temporal distinction. So the virgins might be either slaves or the daughters of the wealthy; by chance a servant might even act alongside her own mistress.

After a few more visits to the grotto with Dario, I saw that he was interested in one girl especially. Furthermore, it was not all on one side. Even during solemn worship, surreptitiously she glanced at him.

Then I discovered that Dario was going to the grotto alone when there were no observances of worship. Rites were usually at dawn, at noon, and at sundown.

"Dario," I protested, "you are laying out for yourself some dreadful trouble. If the god does not revenge himself, our master will."

He was contemptuous. "Gods who do not exist are powerless to hurt," he said. "And Philemon will not know."

"Never let this go further than a look between you," I had to say. "Judgment would be swift as a bolt of lightning."

"Fool," he said. "A look? Shall I tell you something?"

"Yes," I said, too curiously.

"It has gone further already. It is easy in the crypt when the priest is away."

"Dario!" I gasped. "Do you know what this means? What of the other girl, does she know?"

"She watches above, in case someone comes."

"But what of their vows? The virgins are forsworn ..."

Dario laughed in my face. "You make the claim that Mithra exists, and should strike me with a bolt of lightning. Here I stand, safely." He spread his arms. "You also speak of virgins and vows. Do you not understand, there are no virgins? So, no vows!"

I could not make reply.

"You are a fool," he said to me. "Next time you will come with me. You too will have a virgin, as you call them."

I walked away from Dario. Such unashamed corruption of the reverence due to Mithra went beyond my understanding. I needed time to think.

How could the faith in which Philemon believed— not alone myself, but Philemon the master—be so questioned by a stable boy? Questioned? No—absolutely denied and scorned! Mithra, the great god who ruled the heaven and earth and the living and growing things, was being violated in his own most holy sanctuary. Was Dario, a stable boy, stronger than Mithra? And the girls —the sworn virgin girls who it seemed were not virgins at all—how could they, mere women, so flagrantly desecrate the altar they were sworn to keep sanctified with the holy fire?

Mithra lost for me some of the gloss of illusion. Never again could I think quite so highly of the God of Light who would permit such an outrage against him. The specter of doubt had crossed my faith. I wished that I could discuss these things with Persilio, but of course that would be impossible. I had to face alone the creeping suspicion which Dario had bred.

I continued my studies with Demetris the teacher and Spyridus the clerk. Now Archippus, son of Philemon, began to give me small jobs of work to do in the warehouses. Sometimes I weighed and counted bales of wool; at other times I made copies in the fine penmanship I was developing of lists of the goods in stock. The work should have been interesting to me.

All this while the doubt of Mithra and of his ally the Sun God grew within me like a cancer. I knew that Dario returned to the grotto frequently, and I tried to imagine the scene there. Then, shuddering with horror, I put these imaginings from my mind. Each day I continued to go to noontime worship, often in the company of Persilio.

The time approached for Persilio and me to take the first of the seven steps of initiation into the religion of Mithra. We had agreed long before that we should do this together. To achieve the first rank—Corax, or the Raven who announces the new day to come—we would be bound and blindfolded and led through a wall of fire. Afterward we would receive the cleansing bath of the blood of the bull.

Yet now I hesitated to take the initial rite. I was too much confused. The mysteries of the god had lost their reality for me. Was this a phase of my own I was passing through, from which I would emerge with faith as strong as Philemon's? Or was this the end, from which I would go on to think that life was a meaningless existence—without reason or purpose?

I felt that I had to know for certainty.

The desire of knowing led me to do what I never would have done with a sensible mind. One day Dario said to me, "You fool, why do you not come with me this afternoon to the grotto of Mithra? My virgin is there. I shall have her, and you the other one."

"No, no!" I cried out. "You profane heaven itself!"

"I am not thinking of heaven, but of joy in that grotto."

"Dario, I—I cannot believe this. These things you say are lies. You only try to tease and confuse me."

He moved his shoulders. "You think I lie? I am just boastful then? Well, you will come with me today and see. I will show you what one of your virgins looks like under her shroud. Then you will call me a liar, yes?"

"No," I said, "not then."

We walked together through the streets of Colassae and up the hill at the edge of the town. I remember the dust from a camel train moving out to the East. I had helped Spyridus load goods for that shipment. Now the clerk thought I was engaged in listing bills for the materials sent away. No matter, he would not miss me and the bills could be done later.

Cypress trees were darker than usual against the sky above the grotto's entrance. I paused. I knew already that this afternoon was to come to a terrible ending.

"I am going no further," I said to Dario. "I am too uneasy."

"You are coming," he said, and he held my arm. "I will not have anyone tell me I lie. You must learn."

"I will believe you now. . . ."

"No!"

The stable boy would not free me. We continued walking, slowing down at the entrance to the cave. After a moment's pause we entered. The inner room was silent and dark, with slight rays of daylight falling through the entry. The temple smelled of smoke.

Dario tapped a signal with his sandal on the stone floor.

After a moment, a slight figure in white appeared on

the stairs. Slowly she came up from the crypt, and I trembled from knowing at last the truth.

She advanced to Dario, yet all the time gazing at me.

"He will say nothing," Dario said, pointing at me. "He has come for your friend below."

The girl shook her head doubtfully. "She may not," she replied. "She repeats her vows to herself again and again. Perhaps I am the only one who breaks faith."

What the girl said marked itself on my mind. *The only one who breaks faith,* she said of herself. No, she was not the only one. All of us in the sacred temple of Mithra were breaking faith at that moment. The idea haunted me later.

"We'll go down," Dario said to her eagerly. "The priest is away?"

She nodded, and I saw her face clearly in the pale light. She had a sad pensive beauty. It occurred to me that the girl was sincerely in love with Dario. He cared nothing for that, and she herself knew it. Yet she was ready to give herself, her soul and body, her vows and her faith, in a blind gesture. Why? I did not know then. I am no more certain that I know now.

At that moment I turned and fled from the grotto. I ran not knowing where I was going. I fell down beside the hillside path, and found myself clutching a rock where I laid my head and gave myself up to sobs. Tears poured from my eyes, and I was lost in misery.

I may have remained there a long time, or perhaps only a short time. I lifted my head at a sound near me. The red-robed priest of Mithra stood watching me. With him were three or four men, one of whom was Archippus. Behind them were four soldiers.

Inside myself I felt my blood dry as if it turned to ashes. I could not move or make a sound with my voice. The stares of that silent group, all fastened on me, were as hard as the points of the soldiers' swords.

After a moment the priest uttered one word and led

the party on again toward the grotto. They moved swiftly, without speaking. I watched them, and the horror within me rose like an icy wind. I wished to call out, but could not. It was too late in any case. I saw the priest reach the portico and enter in, followed by the others. I heard one terrified cry, then silence—a long, terrible silence that clamped itself over the grotto, the hillside, and the far distant mountains. A bird flew in the sky. An insect chirped in the grass.

Had I tried to run, my legs would have failed. Intuitively I also knew that flight would have spelled a certain doom.

At last the sound came, that for which I must have been waiting. First, a short, sharp shriek that had no human likeness. Then a long wavering wail of death ascending from the grotto's crypt, a cry that pierced the stones and trees and sky. The cry went on and on and on—and faded at last into silence again.

Again I waited while my heart pounded in fear. Perhaps a half-hour passed. Then the four soldiers appeared from the grotto, and then Archippus and the other men. Dario was between two soldiers, his hands bound behind his back. And the virgin too—not the friend of Dario but the other whom I had not seen. Her robes of duty had been stripped from her, and she wore the under-tunic that would not in normal circumstances have been seen out of doors by any man. Her hair fell disarrayed across her shoulders, and she moved as one who has no feeling in her body.

The group drew near, and I hoped would pass me by. I clung to the comfort of the rock. But Archippus simply raised his hand. "Come," he said.

I followed.

We returned to Colossae, and there the group dispersed. The girl was led in shame between two soldiers to her home. I was later to learn that she was the daughter of a freedman, a Roman citizen of good standing.

She had done no deed of her own, except to act as an unwilling accomplice in the desecration of the temple. Each time she had waited in the upstairs room while Dario and the second virgin were in the crypt. Her crime was great enough, but her punishment was mostly to be in her own conscience for the rest of her life.

The other girl had been a slave serving as one of the guardian virgins. Her master was of the group with Archippus. He gave the order for the justice that was done. With soldiers holding her arms, she was laid against the altar, face to the ceiling. A dagger cut her throat, and her blood was allowed to flow out over the altar to cleanse the enormity of the crime against the Gods of Sun and Light. Dario told me long after how it was done in the presence of them all. "It took so long," he sobbed. "They made her feel the dying so!" And the priest sprinkled drops of her blood into the sacred fire as propitiation, and afterward he washed the altar with holy water.

Dario and I were led back to the villa of Philemon by Archippus and the soldiers, and there Dario was delivered into the hands of Zalgrebbo. I was severely questioned, not only by Archippus but by Philemon himself. To my eternal gratitude, the three others in the case had absolved me completely from complicity. The daughter of the freedman swore the truth, that she had never seen me in her life. And the slave, before she died, told how I ran away aghast from Mithra's grotto. Dario, too, took the blame from me.

I was whipped with thirty lashes. Because I was still so young, I was spared far worse.

The stable boy was stripped and bound upon a table. With a knife Zalgrebbo castrated him, so that Dario would never commit that crime again. The thing was done in the presence of every man of Philemon's, as warning for their own behavior.

One might have thought the tale was told, that Mithra's pride was satisfied.

It was not so.

III

Perhaps I could have trusted again in Mithra. The god had been placated with blood, and once more he reigned supreme. Those who dared profane his sacred sanctuary had met their punishment.

I say, perhaps I *could* have trusted again in Mithra. Yet I am not certain. I tried not to let myself think that atonement for their sins had been meted out to the transgressors not by the god but by men. How the priest knew when to lay the trap for Dario and the girl I never knew. Someone must have told. At least, I did not believe that any miracle of divine revelation had come to Colossae. Gossip, or jealousy, had betrayed the sinners. Why had not the god himself intervened, rather than leave settlement of the matter to human chance?

However, I understood that the ways of gods were unfathomable. I did my best to accept Mithra once more as the great hero, invincible and inviolate. I wanted to take the first step of initiation into the holy rites. I said this to Persilio, who agreed that it was time.

But Persilio had not been well. He had become thinner than ever, and one day he failed to appear for his morning class. I waited for him in the villa courtyard where we met each day, and when he did not come I went to the corridor of his apartment. There I was told only that Persilio had been ill through the night. I was not to see him. The faces were long.

What a heavy-hearted morning, that one of Persilio's illness! It was true that closeness of spirit still existed between the two of us. I could not bear to think of him lying ill, in pain and torment, while I who had been as close as a brother remained strong.

The teacher Demetris understood. He went to his window and looked out for a long time while I watched him anxiously.

"I had a dream," he said finally. "Persilio returned to earth from the slopes of Olympus. He looked at us but did not speak."

"You talk as if he were dead!" I cried. "Do not say such things as this."

"It was a dream," he repeated. "Onesimus, we shall do no more work today. Shall we go into the street and walk?"

"Yes," I said. I was filled with foreboding at the words of the teacher. Usually he was a man of practical mind, concerned only with the learning he passed on to his students. I knew that he remained faithful to the Hellenic gods of his ancestors—Zeus, Apollo and the others—but especially to Athena, goddess of wisdom, for Demetris had spoken at times of his worship of Athena. Persilio and I had been amused at his devotion to a figure whom we were taught in Philemon's household to ignore. To us, the teacher's belief gave him a ludicrous aspect.

This morning Demetris did not seem ludicrous. We walked out together on the street, the old man with his long beard, and I taller and bigger-shouldered, with face still soft and hairless. For one aging, the teacher stepped firmly and quickly. I was surprised that I had to walk so fast to remain by his side.

The city was active. A great wagon drawn by oxen rolled past, a chariot pulled by two white horses thundered over the paving stones, and a group of children with hoops dodged in and around the people on foot.

We saw two Romans in togas, moving with dignity through the sunlight in spite of their warm clothing. A woman went by with an empty jar to fetch water; a beggar held out his hand.

"There is much to see," the teacher said. "I find a meaning in people coming together, then separating. Each person leaves something of himself impressed on another, no matter how brief the meeting."

"You have left much impression on Persilio and myself," I said.

"I have impressed learning," he said. "But there is more. Because of me, because of Persilio, because of Apphia and Philemon, you are now yourself. There will be many more persons in the future. After each new meeting you will be renewed, you will become somehow a little altered in one way or another."

"I can understand what you say," I told him. "I gain by every experience."

"Whether you gain or whether you lose is your decision to make."

"How can I know at the time what is good or what is bad?"

"By wisdom. Through wisdom you will separate the grain from the chaff. In doing so you will gain more wisdom."

I waited for Demetris to go on, expecting more. We continued walking. A dog trotted by busily. The streets were crowded with shoppers at the markets, and lazy smells of sun-warmed fruit came to me.

"There," Demetris said, pointing to a house on a corner, "is the home of Abel, the Christian."

"I have heard of Christians," I said. "In the servants' quarters I heard them being discussed. Who are Christians?"

"Followers of a teacher named Christ, of the Jews. He taught a heresy of the Hebrew faith."

"What is the Hebrew faith?"

"They worship the god Jehovah."

Rashly I asked a question I should have left alone. As a question, it was too big for me to ask, but it was one that suddenly entered my mind.

"There are so many differences in beliefs," I said. "How does one really know the true religion?" Then remembering my former uncertainty of Mithra's divine existence, I hurried on, "Indeed, how can one be sure there *is* a true religion?"

Demetris stopped and turned to me. "I spoke before of wisdom," he said. "Now I will speak to you of faith. If I may hold wisdom in one hand and faith in the other, I will be a great man."

"What is faith, that I could hold it in my hand like a stone?"

"Not like a stone," Demetris said, "but like a jewel of glowing quality, into which one may gaze deeply. Then one can believe without reasoning. The essence of faith is absolute acceptance of the unseen and unknown."

I thought that Demetris talked strangely now. I made little attempt to understand him.

We continued walking in silence. Then abruptly the teacher said, "After this you will learn alone. You must have strength. I wish you good fortune."

I stared at him aghast. "What are you saying?" I asked.

He replied, "I think they will not be sending you to me any more."

"But why? Persilio and I. . . ."

The teacher Demetris clasped me suddenly in his arms. "I will pray for you to the goddess Athena," I heard him say. And he was gone, vanished, lost in the crowd on the street.

I know I stood dumfounded, like a lout, scratching my head. What was in the man's mind, I wondered. I shrugged my shoulders, and walked home. On the way I kept wondering if the old man with his talk of Athena was out of his senses.

But on my return I found the whole villa in sad silence. The servants whispered. Even the dogs seemed to be keeping quiet. Persilio had taken a severe turn for the worse, and Philemon had shortly before gone out from the villa with Apphia, no one knew where. Perhaps they sought another physician.

I hurried up the steps to Persilio's apartment. Outside I found Archippus, standing like a statue in stone.

Without speaking aloud, my lips formed the word, "Persilio?"

He raised a hand and made a quick gesture. The meaning was clear. He instructed me to leave, at once.

The hate against me in the eyes of Archippus was beyond measure.

I could not leave so summarily. Tears came to my eyes. Persilio's brother could not have known how I felt.

Archippus stepped forward. He leaned toward me and muttered between his teeth, "Thus Mithra takes his revenge on the family of Philemon, to whom belonged the slave Dario. Had it not been for *you*. . . ."

"No, no!" I choked down my cry.

"Quiet! You will make matters worse. It is what *I* think. Now, go!"

I turned away. Slowly I dragged myself downstairs, through the courtyard and into the street. I found my way across to the edge of the town, and up the hill to the sacred grotto. This visit, so soon after the trouble with Dario, could be misconstrued. If it were thought that I had come now for the same purpose, my lot would be death.

Nothing of that meant anything. I entered the grotto and stumbled down to the crypt. Two virgins were there, on their knees. The priest in his robes was at the altar, chanting. And on one stone bench Apphia and Philemon side by side knelt in prayer.

If they saw me they did not by their motions give any sign of recognition. I went to my usual place at the rear of the crypt. I fell flat on my face on the stone floor in supplication. Quietly, to myself, I sobbed.

The chant of the priest continued. There was no other sound, except when one of the maidens rose to put on the fire another piece of the special pine wood set aside for the purpose, and to fan the flame to brightness.

I prayed for the life of Persilio. I prayed that he could be spared and that I could be taken in his place. I prayed that punishment be placed upon me, where it properly belonged, and not upon the family of Philemon.

What had the teacher Demetris that very morning said of faith? I would believe, without knowing. I promised my faith to Mithra forever, if only he would spare Persilio.

The chanting stopped. I heard the shuffling of feet. Later I looked up. Apphia and Philemon were gone now, and the priest too. The maidens must stay in constant devotion until another pair came to their relief.

Still I prayed. After long hours I rose and walked softly on my sandals from the crypt.

Outdoors, twilight had come to the hillside above Colossae. At the foot of the hill lights glowed in the city. A bird called on its way to roost. The tall cypresses stood dark and still, always with heads bent away from the prevailing wind.

When I returned to the villa of Philemon, I discovered that during the afternoon Persilio had died.

IV

Persilio's death brought the greatest struggle of pain which my body and soul have ever felt. Torments of flogging and fears of dying, even the separations later on from my beloved Aurelia, never were as excruciating as the death of my own and cherished Persilio.

I had loved him as a brother, as if I were of the same blood with him. Through him I had imagined the love of a mother, of a father, and had known the security of being loved. Now as the family gathered together in their grief, they could not share their sorrow with me. I remained outside their smaller circle. I was one alone, one who was a slave, one who should have no feelings or thoughts, one to whom must be denied the comfort of loving and being loved in time of agony.

How I tried to penetrate through the deep black eyes of my master Philemon. How I wished that I could have eased the hurt and the silence of the mother Apphia. Willingly I would have died to bring back into the house the joy that was there when Persilio was alive. I never felt the bonds of slavery as I felt them during that time. It was as though I had chains cutting into my heart. I was Onesimus the useful one, but where was my usefulness? I could do nothing but carry on my work in silence and think the while that my heart beat with tears instead of blood.

After several months the master decided on a trip to Ephesus by the sea to carry goods for trading. It would be an awakening from grief for the family. At first Philemon himself had been as a man crazed. Then he became morose, until he took hold of his senses and went sadly about his business. But Apphia had been as a person bereft of life herself. In the sanctuary of her apartment she found company only with the slave girls who ministered to her and endeavored without avail to rouse her from lethargy.

Yet now we were taking the trip to Ephesus. The master induced Apphia to come from her seclusion and bade her, however unwillingly, to accompany Archippus and himself to the port on the Aegean Sea. To my infinite joy I was selected to go with the family.

Almost begrudgingly Philemon had begun to notice me again. As time went on I could almost imagine a fondness in his expression when he gave me orders. Perhaps I reminded him of Persilio. I tried at least to think that in some way I could substitute for the loss of his son with my loyalty, obedience and service. I knew that a slave boy could never take the place of a father's own son, but any duty I could now render unto Philemon was like a duty given to my lost friend.

Philemon told me that I was to start my active work as his useful steward in business. I was instructed to act as supercargo to the stores of goods being carried to Ephesus, keeping inventory and account of sales as Spyridus did for the entire business.

I was permitted to ride a pony, the better to keep account of the goods moving on the long camel train. The size of the procession was an index to Philemon's prosperity: seventy-five camels fully laden, with drivers, supply men, cooks, and supporting armed guards to protect the shipment from marauders. The guards rode ponies as I did, while Philemon and Archippus were astride handsome horses especially imported from Arabia.

Apphia traveled on a camel in a double-sided saddle especially made for her, with rods and draperies forming a housing over her head and around the four sides. Here she could ride in the manner she wished, sheltered alike from sun's rays and curious eyes. One of her girls stayed with her, while the others rode in their own similar but simpler saddles on following camels.

May one forget the pungency of smells that create memories of a camel caravan? Not when one is a youth alive to adventure, responsive to every new impression. The musk from the hides of pacing animals, the hot leather, the dung, the sweet scents of oriental cargo bales under the sun, the acrid sweat of drivers' bodies, the blowing sand, and the fresh purity of the wind across the dunes—they unite with memories of sounds and sights like the glow of night fires before the camping tents.

I enjoyed watching the changing scenery and talking with the soldiers as we moved slowly over the sandy tracks at camel's pace. I had much time of my own to think, and yet I did not wish to think. I longed for the release of sadness which I hoped to find at Ephesus. Then, as the journey progressed, a restlessness took hold of me. Perhaps being miserable for so long a time had brought about this state. And in spite of myself, I was disturbed by the attitude of Archippus, about which I have so far said little.

Archippus had told me plainly to avoid him except on details of business, for he still held me a partial cause of the death of Persilio. But in retrospect I could not believe that I must share the blame, much as I may have helped to enrage the god Mithra. On the contrary, I myself felt aggrieved and angry that Mithra had paid no attention to my prayers for Persilio. The god had ignored the sincerity and earnestness of my supplications. Mithra, the all-powerful, I was convinced, could have saved the life of my friend. In the greatest hour of tragic need, the deity had failed to listen.

I understand now that injured feelings contributed as

much to my resentment as anything else. If such an attitude be called naïve, it must be remembered that I was young. And far wiser men than I have often made demands on their gods for personal favor, as witness Philemon himself.

I became aware of this truth one morning while the caravan trailed over the grassy plains of western Phrygia. I was riding on my pony some way apart from the rest, shortly after breaking camp. I had already traversed the line of camels, making the routine check to determine that none of the valuable cargo had disappeared during the darkness. The master on his great white horse with blue velvet trappings left his accustomed place by Apphia's side and cantered over to me. He reined in his mount and our animals walked together. I glanced timorously at Philemon, considerably above my height on the pony. The master's dark face was furrowed, and he stared thoughtfully toward the blue haze of the distant mountains.

"Onesimus," he said at last, "the useful one."

"Sir," I replied formally, "I am thrice honored in the service of my master."

"Yes, yes," he said impatiently. "You are becoming older. You will mature much on this journey."

"I will learn as befitting your trust in me."

"I have been pleased with you, Onesimus. You have shown yourself deserving of my trust. Now I wish to talk with you on a subject sore in my heart. You will reply to me with the words of a man, Onesimus."

"May the words of my mouth be always humble," I said, quoting my teacher Demetris.

"I will speak of Persilio," he said.

I was startled. In deference to the grief of the master and the mistress, not one of the household had mentioned Persilio's name.

"You were a friend to my son," Philemon continued.

"I believe you were more fond of him than the circumstances of your association might have required."

It was put as a question. I replied, "He was the only friend I have ever had. I am grateful to you for allowing me to study with him."

Philemon uttered an exclamation of impatience. "You evade me. Speak straight. You must have thought about Persilio's death." He turned his fierce gaze down on me. "I saw you that day in the grotto. You prayed for Persilio."

I looked at my pony's ears. "Yes, sir," I said in a low voice.

"I prayed, too," he said. "Apphia and I prayed that our son's life might be spared. Our prayers were not heeded."

Philemon was waiting for me to say something. I swallowed hard. "I—I think that Mithra was that day busy elsewhere," I stammered.

"You think that he was busy elsewhere?" Philemon roared. His horse pranced nervously. "How can you believe that the all-powerful, all-mighty God of Light, could be too busy to hear our most fervent supplications when the boy lay dying?"

"I do not know," I replied in misery.

"Have you thought about it?"

"Yes," I whispered, "I have thought about it."

"And you concluded that the god to whom we prayed was too busy to hear? Did you remember that I too prayed? I, Philemon, merchant of Colossae?"

"I was thinking more of myself," I said. "With a slave, the god might be preoccupied elsewhere."

I could see that my answer did not satisfy Philemon. He remained silent for a moment. Seemingly my master had reached no better conclusion than I had myself.

Then he looked at me with his burning black eyes, and his black beard seemed to stiffen in his inward agony. Without more words he spurred his horse and in a sudden roar of hoofbeats was away in a flying gallop. On the white steed he raced out from the caravan track across the grass-covered dunes, a cloud of sand hanging in the air behind him. I could see the breeze whip at his cloak and mantle so that at length he gave an appearance of flying through the distance on moving wings.

The captain of the soldiers was alarmed. He turned quickly to Archippus. I did not hear the latter's answer, but I guessed it from the quick motion of Archippus' restraining hand. The son knew well that his father would resent protecting guards hovering over his solitude.

After a time I noticed a clump of the red poppies that grow in profusion on the greener parts of that barren land. I leaned from my saddle to pick one blossom. Then I put my pony into a brief trot and carried the flower to the side of Apphia's camel. The shelter on the animal's back concealed my mistress completely from view behind the curtains.

Archippus rode on the other side of the camel. He stared at me coldly, without speaking.

"My mistress, most humbly I present myself to thee," I called. "I am Onesimus, hoping for your word."

At first nothing happened. Then the heavy hangings parted slightly. The face of Flavia, one of Apphia's serving girls, appeared from the shadows. Her lively black eyes looked down at me.

"Tell our mistress that Onesimus is here," I said. "Onesimus offers to her a blossom of the simplest flower, so Apphia may know of the beauties of the land through which we pass."

I held up the single bloom of red poppy. The hand and bare arm of the girl reached out through the draperies. I noticed the bracelets that jangled from her wrist, and that her skin was white as milk and the shape of the arm delicate and lovely.

"I will tell our mistress," the girl replied. She took

the flower as I stood in my stirrups to hold it up. The curtains fell shut again.

I waited a long time while the pony matched the camel's methodical pace. The creaking of leather, the countless hoofbeats, the snort of the ponies made up the endless combined sound of the camel train. Talk among the soldiers and drivers lagged in the monotony of the continuous march under the hot sun. And on the other side of my mistress's camel Archippus rode on in grim silence.

After a while the curtains parted again and the darting black eyes returned. Flavia spoke softly.

"Our mistress is glad to have the flower that speaks of the beauty of the land," she said. "She wants Onesimus to know that it pleases her."

The pause that followed was filled by the black eyes giving me a message of their own. I tossed my head proudly, and slowly the curtains closed.

I trotted my pony away, feeling older and better than I had for a long time.

The rooftops of Ephesus grew out of the haze early one afternoon. We camped that night near the city and the following morning made ready to enter. Approaching it from the surrounding hill slopes, the town for me had a quality of gold set against the vast blueness of the sea.

Our road led us near the temple of Artemis, sometimes called Diana. The height and glory of it came upon us suddenly as our camels rounded a turn. The temple was raised above the ground on a high foundation from which gleaming marble columns carried the roof into the sky. It dazzled my eyes. I gasped.

I remembered my teacher Demetris' description of the temple at Ephesus. The history of the city for a thousand years had been linked with worship of Artemis, virgin-mother of all life and source of the earth's production. The great edifice built for her had stood in its present splendor for three and a half centuries, from the time of Alexander the Great of Macedonia who had aided with money for its construction.

The shrine, considered one of the wonders of the world, was supposed to surpass in beauty even the splendid temples of Rome itself. I thought that the goddess honored by such glory of architecture must indeed have endeared herself to the hearts of men. The temple was the tribute of many generations of this large and prosperous city. What power did Artemis, called also Diana, possess for its inhabitants?

Our camel train wound its ways through the gates of Ephesus into the narrow streets. The sights of the city distracted me almost to the point of forgetting my responsibilities. It was a place of colors, marble white and pink, azure mosaics, red and yellow tile. Wide avenues were lined with statues of the city heroes on marble pedestals. There were buildings of architectural splendor, parks, and a theater of great size. The people were different from those I had known, including large numbers of Greeks and Jews, Africans, and fair-haired men and women from the North.

This time was in the first years of the Caesar Nero's rule. The glory of Rome was brighter than it had ever been before in its long history. To Ephesus, the great Imperial port, came ships from across the world. By the waterfront for the first time I saw masts and sails, heard the shouts of seamen and stevedores, noticed a vessel move out to sea and another come in across the harbor. There were galleys manned by banks of oarsmen, war vessels, fishing smacks. My imagination leaped at this evidence of the vast commerce of the Empire.

My master and mistress, with Archippus, proceeded to the house of a friend named Julius Andricus, where we of Philemon's close servants were also to stay. I followed the camels to the warehouse arranged for in advance by Philemon. This warehouse adjoined a wharf on the harbor. My work was to begin in earnest now, for in my care was the inventory of the entire caravan cargo: the bales of wool, bundles of silks, chests of gems, bars of silver, the spices and foodstuffs.

As our camels came in to be unloaded along one side of the warehouse, passengers were descending on the other side from a vessel which we were told had just arrived from Greece. I noticed a Roman citizen in toga accompanied by his retinue. I was too busy to pay much attention, but suddenly I was aware of the Roman standing before me.

He was of medium height, and he had a large nose highly bridged, a thin mouth, and darting eyes. One of his hands hung at his side; the other was lost in the toga folds over his chest.

"I am Vergilio Pontius, trader of Rome, arrived here from Athens," he told me. "I assume by your still-loaded camels that you are bringing goods to Ephesus from the interior."

I paused to reply, "That is right, master. This is the caravan of Philemon, merchant of Colossae, accompanied here by him in person."

"I seek wares to take back to Italy," the trader said. "If your master is interested in selling, I will be pleased to discuss matters with him."

"Sir, indeed, I will tell Philemon of your interest," I said. "He stays in Ephesus at the house of Julius Andricus, his friend."

"I will communicate with him," the merchant said.

He turned to his retinue standing a little behind him. Among them were a man and a girl in the attire of higher classes.

"Aeneas," the trader Vergilio called, "I have need of you."

I had time for only the briefest glimpse of the girl. I was surprised, I remember, by her uncovered head and by the Italian-style tunica so different from Phrygian dress.

For an instant her eyes caught mine. They were blue, wide, and accentuated by heavy dark lashes. She looked at me openly and frankly, without the shyness typical of the girls of our country. Her head was held high, her shoulders erect and proud. Her attitude was not bold, but self-confident.

The trader's man Aeneas came up, deferentially. "Service, master," he said.

"This is the freedman Aeneas," Vergilio told me. "He acts for me in business. You may trust his word."

"Yes, master," I replied. "I am Onesimus, steward to Philemon. I will act at my master's bidding."

Vergilio looked at me more closely. "You are young," he said. "I have heard the reputation of Philemon. You must be capable beyond your years, else Philemon would not trust you with his stewardship."

"Thank you, master," I said.

The trader turned to Aeneas. "Perhaps the steward to Philemon will give you their list of goods available. You know in what we are interested." He added to me, "Advise your master we look particularly for Phrygian wool."

Vergilio inclined his head briefly and strode off. I saw the girl follow behind him, not at his side as I expected but several paces to the rear. The servants in turn followed her.

I could not resist the opportunity. "Who is she?" I asked Aeneas.

"She is by name Aurelia, slave to Vergilio. She is a musician, and she travels with the master in order to entertain his guests. Are you ready to proceed?"

"Yes," I replied.

Philemon gave me much liberty during our stay in Ephesus. I was free to wander through the streets and watch the great activity of the port. I spent hours on the wharves, drank wine with sailors, and mingled with townspeople on the avenues. I enjoyed myself, absorbing knowledge of this new world.

In Ephesus, as in Rome, the dress of slaves did not differ in any way from the plain attire of tradespeople or freedmen. No one necessarily took me for a slave, and it would not have mattered if they had. Here, as elsewhere throughout the Empire, slaves numbered nearly half the population. In fact, the freedom allowed by my master was no more unusual than it would have been in Rome itself. Like most slaves, I was always granted a pittance of coins with which to pay my own way.

The first day I visited the temple of Artemis from curiosity. I was impressed, and to some extent troubled. I could not avoid the impression of the perpetual power of the goddess of the city. In all its thousand-year history Ephesians had worshipped the deity of nature. The sincerity of the people's faith, as I myself saw it, could not be tossed lightly aside.

I saw those in distress and need come before the great statue of the goddess in the sanctuary of the temple. In almost every case they left the shrine with reassured faces. It was hard for me to reconcile such faith with the scorn I had been taught to hold against all such gods during my youth in Philemon's household. Then my instruction led me to revere only Mithra. But Mithra had failed the family of Philemon on the day of need. Were, after all, the legendary gods and goddesses the true ones?

I left an offering of money in the temple of Artemis to be on the safe side.

It was easy for me to understand why so many people, confronted by such puzzles, gave up belief in any religion. The answers were too difficult for them to find.

On that very same day an event occurred which finally convinced me of the falsity of religious belief. My mind was prepared to accept the premise, and needed only the excuse. It came within an hour of leaving the temple of Artemis.

I walked by a group of five or six persons engaged in a street-corner discussion. Voices were loud. One young man was holding his own in a violent argument with the others. I slowed down to listen and watch.

"Then what do you say of Cybele, and of Apollo and Venus?" one of the group demanded angrily. "Listen carefully now—what do you say of Artemis of Ephesus, in whom is placed the trust of our city?"

The young man remained unperturbed. His eyes twinkled in spite of the array against him. He was tall, fair-skinned but dark-haired. I guessed that he was of Phrygian origin.

"Jehovah has said that there shall be none other gods but him," he replied easily.

"Yet you yourself speak of another god, this man of Jerusalem whom you describe? Jehovah is God of the Jews, but the one you tell of has been killed by the Jews."

"In accordance with the prophecies. The one of whom I speak is the Son of God, sent by the Father to redeem the sins of the world."

"How could he redeem sins by being crucified?" another scoffed. "He could not save himself."

"By his act he sacrificed himself for the sins of mankind. He who believes in him is redeemed from sin."

Although I realized that the discussion was on some religious matter, I had no understanding yet of what was said. I drew closer to the circle, seeing no harm in listening.

"Is this the teaching of the one called Paul?" asked an old man.

"Paul of Tarsus, apostle, teaches the word of Jesus Christ."

"He performs miracles I hear," cried another. "He has done so even in Ephesus."

The young man folded his arms and smiled.

"You may call them miracles," he told his audience. "We say they are results of faith in God. Through the hands of Paul, our God hath wrought miraculous things in Ephesus for those who believe in him."

"I would like to hear the teaching of this Paul of whom I have heard much," said the old man. "Where would I find him?"

"At the school of Tyrannus," the young man said. "He is there each day for those who will come."

"And who are you?" demanded another. "Are you also one of the Jews?"

"I am Epaphras of Colossae, like yourselves a native of these parts of Asia. Yet one and all we are alike in the sight of God."

The Ephesians muttered among themselves. Two shrugged and walked away, and the old man also left after saying he would attend Paul. Those remaining glared angrily at the young man who had dealt with them in such assured manner.

"I think," one said, "you are speaking against Artemis, the goddess savior of our city. Those of us who call ourselves Ephesians will not feel kindly toward such insults."

"I speak only for one God," Epaphras answered sharply. "Know you now the way to true redemption!"

The three men moved away, talking among themselves. They kept glancing back, still muttering.

Seeing the young man alone, I went to him.

"Epaphras of Colossae," I said, "I am Onesimus, also of Colossae, recently come to Ephesus. Perhaps you will have a cup of wine with me?"

He seemed pleased to see me. "A cup of wine with pleasure, sir. You can tell me the latest news of our town."

We went to a little shop where we could sit together. Over our wine I told him gossip of our home, and news of Philemon and Archippus, of whom he knew. At the same time I examined him curiously, noting his shabby clothing.

At last I could restrain myself no longer. "You are a Christian," I said. "I have never talked with one before."

If he thought I was facetious, he gave no indication. "There are few Christians at Colossae."

"Oh," I said, "I have heard of Christians."

"The message of Christ spreads far," he answered.

"The cult of the Christians is new, is it not? I have been told that it arose from Jerusalem in recent times."

Epaphras paused to count on his fingers. "How long ago? Yes, it would be thirty years now—or nearly that —since Jesus taught. There have been many converts since. You will find Christians in many places, and continually more. Christ's disciples travel from one end of the world to the other, baptizing and carrying the presence of the Holy Spirit."

I could see that my new acquaintance was fanatically prejudiced in favor of the sect. But this earnestness of his suddenly had a devastating effect. All at once I was reminded of the earnestness of Mithra's followers, even to the virgins spending long hours on their knees in painful prayer. I thought of the sincere wisdom and experience of Demetris explaining the reality of the gods of Greece. And only an hour before I had been impressed by the devotion of the Ephesians in the temple of Artemis.

I came to an instant conclusion, even as Epaphras spoke. All religions were alike. They were traps to catch the naïve, the gullible, the fools. This Christian had made it plain to me.

". . . because the doctrine of Christ has a meaning for all people," Epaphras was saying. Quickly I brought my thoughts back to listen to him. "If you would hear Paul himself, you would understand the promise of God's forgiveness of sin, and the glory of eternal life."

I laughed. I should not have done that. I did not mean to be rude to a new friend. It was because of the trend of my thoughts and the sudden relief at coming to an end of my inquiries.

Epaphras stared at me. Two spots of angry color appeared on his cheeks.

"Please do not be offended," I said hastily. "I must tell you with frankness that I cannot believe in your Christ, not any more than I can believe in the power of Mithra or the holiness of Diana. They are different only in the matter of names and procedure. Oh, I know, I have studied them! I had faith once, and I have lost it so that I can believe in nothing. . . ."

I stopped. My voice had risen. People inside the wineshop turned their heads. Epaphras' hand tightened. I wondered if he were about to strike me.

"Ah!" he cried. "You are one of those for whom we search especially. Our disciples who pass through the fires of doubt are the greatest in the service of Christ. You can be chosen for great things, like Paul himself! You must come at once with me to find him. . . ."

"What!" I rose to my feet. "I told you that I will have none of it, and yet you answer so? I should not have spoken to you in the beginning. Forgive me, and good day."

I left a coin from my pittance for the wine and strode quickly away. I did not look back at all, knowing that I had left my fellow Colossean dumfounded.

I convinced myself that I had gained a victory. Henceforth I was to be independent of idle gods and their priests. The pomp and pretexts of religion I could scorn at my free will. The doubts and fears of divinities I could shake out of my mind.

V

The Roman trader Vergilio Pontius received Philemon and Archippus at the house he hired for his visit in Ephesus. He gave a banquet in their honor, following successful business discussions. I was received also, as my master's steward. According to custom, I took my position standing at a brief distance behind Philemon's couch.

Other guests were present with their slaves. In rank Vergilio and Philemon occupied center couches, with Archippus next. Aeneas, being a freedman employed by Vergilio, took a couch to one side. Those of us standing at the back of the room partook likewise of the banquet after our masters were served.

I looked for the girl Aurelia, but in vain at first. Only after the completion of the meal and the serving of much wine did Vergilio give a signal. At that, she appeared.

I gasped when I saw her. She was dressed in a white tunic fringed with gold, and a gold band circled the coil of dark hair on her head. The tunic hung loosely, but a sash binding her waist revealed a remarkable slimness. Brooches of brilliant jewels held the tunic at the shoulders, and gold sandals scarcely hid the delicacy of her small feet.

She crossed the room demurely and with grace, carrying a lyre. As she passed me, she looked up and met my gaze. There was the briefest light of recognition in the blue eyes under the dark lashes, and she smiled. I had a strange feeling of weakness and exhilaration, as if for the first time a curtain had parted and I had a glimpse of a meaning of life not before dreamed.

Aurelia moved out before the guests. At a nod from her master she began to play on the lyre, and she sang in a voice soft and full. Her themes were lyrics of ancient Athens, pleasing to hear. I remained spellbound watching her, noting the rhythm of her fingers over the strings and the swelling of her throat as she sang.

She must have been aware of my enraptured attention, for she looked in my direction several times. The guests were entertained, too, and they were loud in their praise at the end of each piece. Archippus especially showed himself vocal, for by now he was full of much wine.

I had never listened to music like this. The house of Philemon was barren of the arts, for the master's temperament responded little to such appeals. I had heard the formal chants in the grotto of Mithra and the unrestrained music and song of the streets of Colossae. Demetris in his old cracked voice had given to Persilio and me some examples of the lyric odes, and Persilio himself had before his death become interested in instrument playing. Yet all these were scarcely even preludes to the beautiful renditions of the girl Aurelia.

She finished at last, to my disappointment. At a further signal from Vergilio she went to the couch of Archippus and sat on the floor beside him. She placed her elbows on the seat of the couch and talked to him with much animation. Archippus began to smooth the shining darkness of her hair with his hand, and she presented no objections. She made no protest even when his fingers moved over the whiteness of her neck and shoulders.

The wine cups of the guests were kept steadily full. Archippus was losing his senses, but Aurelia ignored his stupefied clumsiness. She made conversation that he could scarcely answer, and I writhed within myself from the unfamiliar sensation of jealousy. I wished to strike his hand to keep the wandering fingers from her body.

I knew that I had no rights of my own except for the salvation of my soul, for I was owned completely by Philemon. The earthly destiny of a slave is bound to his master's bidding. Aurelia herself was in a similar situation, for she was slave to Vergilio. I trembled at the implications of that relationship. There was nothing, nothing, at all possible for me as regarded Aurelia.

Yet during the aftermath of that banquet I threw behind me every logical restraint and every reason of sound mind. I had fallen in love with Aurelia.

I knew it at the time, and I also realized the hopeless folly of it. How far beyond control can human emotions become? I watched her as the banquet began to break up and she leaped lightly to her feet. She ran deft fingers over her hair, tidying it back into place. I felt a wave of surging anger as I saw the way she smiled at the drunken Archippus, and how she held out her hand to him in farewell. She moved to leave the room, but I intercepted her progress. I know my heart beat wildly. I must have had a very red face, and stammered. I could not have presented an admirable picture of prepossessing youth.

Yet she stopped.

"I liked your music," I said. "Is it possible—may I—some time—hear more. . . ."

Aurelia smiled graciously, though in my nervousness I feared her attitude was only condescending.

"Perhaps," she replied. "Will your master bring you here again?"

"I do not mean that. I will come myself. Why do you not want to see me?"

"Oh." Her blue eyes became very wide. She glanced at Vergilio saying farewell to his guests. "My master would not care for me to do that."

"He will not know. Please, tomorrow. . . ."

She hesitated. Then she whispered, "At siesta time. There is a back gate to the garden. You will wait outside."

"Yes, yes," I almost cried aloud.

She was gone.

"Onesimus. . . ."

Philemon was calling. Archippus required help to leave the room, and I placed my arm around the master's son to support him. In such fashion we left the house. Archippus was a dead weight and his head rolled from side to side. He mumbled imprecations against me. None of it mattered. I lived until the morrow.

At the time of siesta I was standing under a palm tree outside the back gate of the garden. I tried to appear unconcerned, but to little avail, especially when Aurelia did not appear. I shifted from one foot to another, walked close past the gate to look through it, and did my best to hear over the wall sounds from the house.

I saw the foolishness of my plan. Even had Aurelia wished to come—and I did not discourage myself from this thought—she would have found it impossible. Custom prohibited male and female slaves of different masters from associating together. The reasons were clear enough. Nothing could ever follow except trouble for the masters. Yet I would not leave the deserted street.

At last the latch clicked. With a swift movement Aurelia was outside, and swung the gate shut behind her.

Instantly all went from my mind except the dark beauty of Aurelia to my eyes, and the pleasure of her presence. I could do no more than stare.

"You are displeased," she said of my silence. "I have kept you waiting."

"No, no," I managed to say, "I was only afraid . . ."

"I was busy," she explained. "My master would not be pleased with me if he knew I were here."

She was clad in long-sleeved white *stola,* or outer tunic, and wore a scarf over her head and shoulders. The oval of her face under the folds of the scarf showed a simple purity of expression. Under her arm she carried the lyre.

"I am glad you have come," I said. "Can you walk with me?"

"Yes, a little way, if I return before the end of siesta. If I am discovered, I will be punished."

"We will return in time. There is a hill not far, and from there we can see the sea. Shall we go?"

She nodded, and walked on at my side through the streets of the town. She had pulled her scarf further over her head to hide her face. I kept stealing glances at her, and felt the pride rising in me because she was with me. I had never before walked abroad with a girl.

We passed through the gate of the town and made our way a short distance up the hillside. Grass grew here, and there was a view over the rooftops toward the sea. We sat near each other, and Aurelia took her lyre and sang to me. Her voice was soft and sweet against the sounds of the open air: the wind over the hill, the hum of insects, and the far bray of a donkey from the town.

I watched Aurelia, and knew that my love must grow forever despite all that lay between us. I felt that this experience would mean as much to me as anything yet to be. That so much of my intuitive foresight of that day has come true for both of us is remarkable.

Aurelia's songs were light and gay at first, and then sad, sung in a haunting way. I asked her, "Are you sad?"

"No," she said, "I only sing as I know the music. Why should I be sad?"

"I am," I said. "I am sad because I am in slavery and am not my own master."

"And I, too, but that is our lot. I will not be sad over my lot."

I frowned. "I am a man," I said. "A woman needs not to belong to herself alone. But for a man it is part of himself in being a man."

"I suppose that is the difference," she said. "If I were not owned by someone, I would not know what I should do. I belong to Vergilio Pontius. Until he bought me, I belonged to a man and woman in Rome who had owned me since I was a small child. They bought me in turn from the centurion who took me from an enemy town north of Italy. I have no feeling of not belonging."

"I have always belonged, too," I told her. "That does not make me happier now."

"What can you do?" she asked. "It is better to be content, as I am."

"You have already belonged to so many people," I said. "Who were the man and woman in Rome who bought you as a child?"

"They were kind to me. They taught me my work. When I was old enough to bring a good profit, they sold me."

"What is your work?"

I was almost afraid to ask the question.

"I am an entertainer. I play music and sing, and I carry on a good conversation."

"Is—that all?"

"No," she said, looking at me frankly, "when I am older I will be a hetaera. I will be the concubine of a Roman, or I may live in a brothel with others like myself. That will depend on who owns me next."

"Perhaps Vergilio will keep you."

"I will be worth too much money. He will have another young girl for his purposes. Vergilio is a trader."

I thought of Apphia, and of the love between her and her husband Philemon. Inevitably I had to compare the two women—the one whom I loved as a son must love his mother, and the other whom I wished to love as a man should love his wife.

Apphia was warm and kind, with the grace and beauty of an older woman. Aurelia was as well-mannered, as beautiful in her way, as educated, but with the inexperienced bloom of youth. Yet Aurelia needed a warmth such as Apphia's. Through no fault of her own, she lacked love.

It was distressing to me that Aurelia as a woman must face a life without love.

"It is my lot," Aurelia said again, as if she guessed my thoughts.

"Women are made for love!" I cried rebelliously. "Where will you find love in such a life?"

"Everywhere," she said. "I will always be loved."

"What kind of love? Not what I mean. . . ."

"Love is love. Is not most love temporary anyway?"

"I suppose Archippus loved you last night."

"I know he did."

"I hated it when he smoothed your hair and shoulders!"

Aurelia laughed. "You must learn, dear Onesimus." It was the first time she had used my name. "You are young, perhaps younger than I."

"I am in my sixteenth year," I said.

"And I in my fifteenth. It was my duty to Vergilio last night to entertain your Archippus. I did not mind the touch of his hand."

I seized her wrist. "Aurelia, there is so much I want to say to you. I—I do not know how to say it. . . ."

"No, no, you must not say it, whatever it is. I will go back now, it is time."

"You will come again with me? Tomorrow?"

"It can lead nowhere. And I will be punished."

"I wish to hear more songs, and perhaps poetry."

"No. . . ."

"Then I can give love too!" I cried, suddenly recklessly. "I'm as good as the others. You must come with me again!"

Aurelia looked at me and her eyes began to fill with tears. I had touched something within her after all.

"I will come tomorrow," she said in a low voice. "By the gate at siesta time, providing my master wills not otherwise."

"Must we always be so subject to the whims of our masters?" I exclaimed in the bitterness of rebellion.

"Yes, always," she replied. "It is as it should be."

She walked home by herself, insisting that it was better to do so. I followed her at a little distance, to be certain of her safety, until she disappeared inside the garden gate.

Aurelia came with me to the hillside three more times. Each time she brought her lyre and softly sang to me the songs of ancient Rome, of the Italian countryside, and the ballads of Athenian heroes.

I cannot imagine how I looked to her on those days. I was uncouth, dressed in plain gray woolen chlamys, with a countryman's sandals. My face grew a soft blond mat that scarcely promised the beard to come. I had the education acquired from Demetris, and manners learned in Philemon's house. Yet compared to all that Aurelia knew of art and literature, philosophy and history, I appeared a dolt. She seemed a jewel of perfection; I a rough lump.

After her music each day, we spoke of many things. She told me of Rome, that fabulous city of power and splendor. She had seen the Caesar, and knew by name certain of the senators. I listened with eagerness to her tales of travels in Italy and Greece, to her descriptions of ships and the sea, and of islands with green-capped mountains. In turn I could tell her of Asia, of the inland cities, and of the way we lived at Colossae. I could teach her about silks and wools, and about jewels and things of which she had never heard.

We spoke of religion. In Ephesus my master Philemon

had learned of the reputation of the Christian teacher, Paul of Tarsus. Twice already Philemon had heard him speak, and each time he returned to Apphia like a man shaken by a great wind. I could not understand it and asked Aurelia what she knew.

There were Christians in Rome, she said. Many of them were Jews who believed that Christ had come to save them from the imminent Apocalypse, the prophesied end of the world. But others than Jews had joined the sect, she thought, although she did not know why.

Aurelia had never spoken with a Christian. She herself worshipped no special divinity, she told me. She did not disbelieve; she was merely unfamiliar with the concept of religious faith. Her teachers had been more concerned with her qualifications for becoming a hetaera than with her soul.

If she could believe in any god, she said, she would prefer Vesta, guardian goddess of Rome. The reason, she admitted, was her sympathy for the Vestal Virgins, the maidens who served in the temple of Vesta through thirty years of self-denial. Only recently one Vestal had been discovered while breaking her vow of chastity, and had been buried alive in sight of the frenzied, shrieking populace of Rome. Aurelia said that she had cried that night—thinking of the wayward girl dying slowly in her lonely tomb.

As we talked of these things, we lay under the afternoon sun on the hillside with tall grass growing around us. Then, on the third afternoon, she made mention of the fact that Vergilio would be gone from Ephesus for the entire following day. He was to take a trip on business to a neighboring town, and Aeneas would go with him.

"Aurelia," I exclaimed. "Then you can come with me for the day. We will go to the sand by the sea!"

She nodded. "Yes, I had thought so. I will tell the

servants I go to the temple of Artemis. They will understand that."

She looked at me with those blue eyes that by now haunted my days and nights, and smiled wistfully. Aurelia, too, was discovering a new kind of warmth in life.

I borrowed a camel from our herd. I set myself right with Philemon by asking his permission to do so. My master did not seem concerned in my plans. He was becoming more obsessed about the Christians, and he expected once more to hear the man called Paul.

Aurelia met me at the paddock near our warehouse. Her tunic was covered by a wool mantle, and over her head was the scarf that shielded her face from busy eyes and from the wind and sun. She laughed when she saw the camel, and I was relieved at her acceptance of the idea. Yes, she agreed, the experience would be unforgettable. I helped her mount while the camel knelt.

To ride a camel has never been the most comfortable proceeding for anyone. We lurched off together through the streets of Ephesus, I guiding the beast and Aurelia sitting behind me, her legs to one side. She had to hold onto me for support, and I felt with pleasure the strength of her hands on my waist.

After a time our bodies fell into the rhythm of the camel's pace. Aurelia talked in lively manner, speaking of the people and the scenes we passed.

Once outside Ephesus, we made our way along the edge of the harbor and past the headlands of the far shoreline. There were farmers' trails for cattle at the edges of the fields, and finally we found where we could go down to the yellow sands along the sea. We rode in the joy of the sunlit day and the tingling of a light breeze from across the water.

We dismounted on the beach and left our camel standing with his own perpetual patience. I clasped

Aurelia to help her down and felt the warmth and subtleness of her body in my hands. She shed the mantle and the scarf, and the sea wind blew the material of her tunic against her legs and breast. We ran across the sand and searched for shells along the edge of the lapping waves.

Then we rested under the shelter of a dune. The sea lay before us and the sun kept us warm. I had brought wine, fruit, and a loaf of bread. We shared the refreshment slowly, enjoying it and the company of each other.

Forgive me, dear Aurelia, for revealing so much about ourselves. I am writing of myself, Onesimus, and of my love for you. That day on the beach near Ephesus became a part of myself. To say that I matured is not enough. I found that rarest thing in life, the perfect communion of two human souls, a thing so fragile and so perfect that one may compare it to the discovery of the most delicate flower. Although the flower itself must wilt and fade away, in memory it remains as vividly alive and beautiful as on the moment it first burst into bloom.

So it was with you, Aurelia. I believe I was not alone in my response to the beauty of those moments. We shared it together. I know that the deeper understanding I gained on that day has had a profound influence on this later life of mine.

We rode very slowly on our camel back to Ephesus. We made the most of each other's presence while yet we could. For Aurelia told me that day, "Onesimus, this beginning for us is already the end."

"What do you mean?" I asked with alarm.

"I did not wish to say it until now. My master Vergilio told me last night that his work in Ephesus is finished."

I turned cold as I waited for her to continue.

"Tomorrow we take a ship for Alexandria, and from there back to Rome."

The blow struck me hard. Of course I had known it had to happen, but one's nature inevitably defers consciousness of the end of all things. Now to accept the realization that we would never meet again was too difficult to bear. No wonder I held the camel to the pace of a turtle. Even so, as the heat of the sun in the west began to cool and the shadows under the pine trees grew perceptibly longer, we reached the gate of Ephesus.

Inside the town something had changed.

The city appeared to be filled with confusion. Men were running through the streets and shops were being closed. Women leaned from windows to look down, and from a further part of the town came the sound of shouting.

"What is it?" Aurelia asked in sudden fright.

"I do not know," I said.

"I must return home quickly," she said. "If my master knows I am out at this hour, he will be very angry."

Our way crossed a wide street which led to the city's amphitheater. Here we found a great crowd. From the height of our camel we could see plainly down the length of the street. Two men bound with thongs were being pushed toward the theater.

"It's like the time in Rome when they took the Vestal Virgin!" Aurelia cried.

I had never seen a mob in action. Men shouted and carried sticks and stones. At the same time I noticed that many of them seemed not to know what they were doing, or why they were there.

We had to halt while the people passed. As we waited another small group appeared out of a neighboring alley. One man led the rest, while those with him pulled at his arms and clothing to hold him. They came very near us. The man in the lead brushed off the restraining hands as if they were nothing. He had the strength of a god; yet he was not a young man. He was smaller than he was large, with a head partly bald and his remaining hair graying. He was dressed plainly, almost crudely, in a gown of dark brown.

He was in a rage, a rage so fierce that it burst forth from him and made the spectator hold his breath. His eyes blazed and the beard on his face shook. He strode forward with such passion that it seemed that not even walls would stand under blows from those clenched fists. The sight of him drove out all one's thoughts except amazement that a man could attain such ferocity of purpose.

What might have happened had he faced that crowd I could not guess. But, under the very nose of our camel, two young men ran up. One I recognized—Epaphras, the Christian from Colossae, with whom I had talked. The other had so kind and gentle a face that he attracted attention even on such a violent occasion as this.

Both saw instantly what was happening. They spread their arms and bore down on the oncoming angry man.

"Master, master!" cried the one named Epaphras. "They will kill you! Return to shelter. . . ."

The angry one ran full into their outstretched arms. "It's Gaius and Aristarchus!" he muttered between clenched teeth. "They need me. . . ."

"You cannot help them," the second man shouted at him. "You can do nothing! The sight of you would inflame them the worse!"

"Listen to Luke," Epaphras urged. "He is right, master."

The two pushed from the front, and the rest of the group behind regained their holds. By sheer strength of opposition, the entire group carried their leader back into the alley, and all of them disappeared.

"Oh!" Aurelia cried behind me, and I felt the shudder through her body.

"They must be Christians," I said. "The strong one could be the man named Paul. Something has happened indeed during this day."

"Let me go," Aurelia begged. "My house is not far from here. Vergilio must not see me with you!"

She freed herself and dropped to the ground from the height of the camel's back. She looked up with a quick smile, and I had time only to lean down for the briefest clasp of her hand.

Aurelia was gone. I was left with the memory of her slight figure under the mantle and shawl hurrying away through the crowd of people running. . . .

I took the camel back to the stable, and walked alone through the streets in a daze. The excited crowds had moved on inside the theater. With a desire to think of something other than the loss of Aurelia, I pushed my way into the arena.

A disorganized mass of people filled the place. I overheard much muttering and questioning: "What is it?" "Who are they?" "What should we do with them?"

And there was loud shouting: "Great is Artemis! Great is Diana of the Ephesians!"

I saw a man jump up upon a platform and try to appease the angry crowd.

"Men of Ephesus!" he cried. "What man is there who knows not that the city of the Ephesians is a worshiper of the great goddess Diana, and of the image which fell down from Jupiter? Seeing then that these things cannot be spoken against, you ought to be quiet and do nothing rashly. For you have brought here these men who are neither robbers of churches or yet blasphemers of your goddess. If Demetrius and the craftsmen who are with him have a grievance, the law is open!"

Over all the crowd came a murmur which I did not understand, not knowing the cause of what was happening.

"If you have anything else in dispute," the speaker urged, raising his voice even higher, "it shall be determined in a lawful assembly. We are in danger of being called in question for this day's uproar. . . ."

The people stirred restlessly, one looking at another as if for the first time. "He is the town clerk," I heard someone explain. "He knows what he means to say. It is best we take his word."

"Go back to your homes and to your shops!" the clerk shouted. "Let this assembly be dismissed, and allow these two men to go their way!"

The atmosphere changed. The malevolent mob became single persons again, each one diffident about his presence here and nervous of the blame of his neighbor. They began to leave the theater, one by one, almost stealthily.

I watched until most had gone. I saw the two men who had been bound released from their thongs. Then, to my astonishment, I saw Philemon. He was standing alone, deeply lost in thought.

I went to him at once. "Master," I said, "what do you do here?"

He looked at me with a glance that seemed not to comprehend that I was there at all. "I saw them attack the Christians, Gaius and Aristarchus," he said with wonderment, speaking as if he were answering his own spirit inside himself. "I have met them both, at the times I have been with Paul. Do you know it was Demetrius, the silversmith, our own customer for bars of silver, who set the people against the Christians?"

"Demetrius?" I asked. "But why?"

Philemon frowned. "Demetrius of Ephesus makes silver images, especially of the goddess Artemis. The Christians preach that there are no gods to worship which can be made with human hands. So great is the influence of Paul and the Christians that in Ephesus and throughout Asia the making of silver shrines to Artemis has fallen away. Neither Demetrius nor any of the silversmiths have business enough to buy our silver. In revenge, Demetrius stirred the people by saying that the Christians blaspheme Artemis!"

"Then the Christians are affecting our business, too," I said.

Savagely Philemon turned on me. "Do you think of business before the redemption of your soul?" he demanded. "Let me tell you of the Christians! This Paul performs miracles. He makes the ill whole, and the blind see." His voice broke. "Had we been Christians when Persilio was sick, the apostles of Christ might have saved him from death, even as the god Mithra did not try!"

"They say that Christ himself died," I said.

He ignored my remark. "Onesimus, my son," he said solemnly, "we will be baptized in the Christian faith— Apphia, Archippus, all of us! We have found in Ephesus a God in whom we can believe!"

I began to tremble.

"Master," I said with difficulty, "forgive me forever. I cannot be a Christian."

The astonishment he showed on his face frightened me even more.

"Are you afraid?" he asked.

"Of—what?"

"Are you afraid of what you have seen this day? You think the smith Demetrius and those with him will persecute you, even as Gaius and Aristarchus today were persecuted?"

"No, master, it is not that I fear. I—I cannot believe."

The sorrow in his face was hard to see. "I called you my son," he said slowly. "But of course you are not my son. I lost my son. You are only Onesimus, the useful one."

His words hurt me and my heart was filled with sadness. I so wished that I could believe in this Christ, if only to please my master. But I could not act a lie to him who gave me of his affection.

Philemon walked toward the entrance of the amphitheater, now nearly empty. I followed at a respectful distance, and we joined the last of the stragglers from the once-disorderly mob.

VI

Shortly after our return from Ephesus, the apostle Paul sent his disciple Epaphras to Colossae. The Christian resided in the household of Philemon as a guest for some weeks, the while he preached and taught in the city. He made many conversions, especially among former followers of Mithra and other Oriental cults who followed the example of Philemon in turning to Christ. A Christian church in Colossae became well established.

Because he was a guest in the house of Philemon, it was impossible for me to avoid Epaphras. He was young enough to be compatible, and he was educated and well-spoken and personable. My status meant nothing. I had many long conversations with him.

I refused steadfastly to be drawn into discussion of religion. Epaphras respected my rights to my opinions. Faith, he said, meant absolute belief, even though the substance of faith lay beyond human reasoning. I did not understand him when he said that faith could not be explained, only accepted. Jesus Christ was the Son of God. His life and resurrection after death might confound human logic; yet only by faith in Christ could one obtain the visitation of the Holy Spirit.

I heard Epaphras speak of Christ to other persons in terms of such clear sincerity that I have wondered since how I guarded my resistance so firmly. "Christ lives!" he said. And most of those who heard believed.

At times I think I feared that Epaphras might be teaching the truth, after all. To my present shame my suspicion only gave me the more incentive to repel the Christian faith. Epaphras was well aware of my attitude even though I remained quiet in his presence. Only once did he speak out to me, repeating in a sense what he had said at Ephesus: "Oh, to you who have such certainty of disbelief, what pity you would not place the same certainty in belief!"

But when the time came for Epaphras to leave, I was sorry to see him go. He had work to do in the nearby town of Laodicea, and later he was to meet Paul who had been traveling in Macedonia. Epaphras had been a companion to me, and his departure left a void that I came to fill in a most unfortunate manner.

First, I must write of Philemon. My master had quite naturally taken over the leadership of the Christian church in Colossae and become its bishop or responsible head. The congregation of Christians met in his home, it being large enough and the church failing to have a place of worship of its own. The grotto of Mithra was deserted by Philemon and Apphia and Archippus now that they believed there were no other gods save Jehovah and his Son.

In fact the worship of Mithra in Colossae fell for the time being on difficut days. Many of the devotees of Mithraic ritual believed Christianity to be a similar theology, and to substitute one for the other required no great effort. The ideals of Christianity were new, and they seemed easier to follow.

I am convinced that even Philemon was swayed by

influences carried over from Mithraism. Initially, I am certain, my master swung to Christianity more in anger against Mithra than in conviction of Christ's divinity as the Son of God. What happened later appears to prove my interpretation.

As leader of the Colossian church, Philemon practiced great diligence. He led the congregation in prayers, assisted in conversions and baptisms, and spread the word of Christ among his business acquaintances and social friends. Long after Epaphras went away, the local church still grew and flourished.

What disgusted me was Philemon's personal response to Christianity. I was accustomed to a master eager in business, quick in temper, fiery in action. Instead of cultivating his own self-pride, he became a meek man. Instead of roaring at a wrong done to him, he was all servility, no longer seeking retaliation. He gave away half of the wealth he had earned so cleverly over the years. He restricted Zalgrebbo in administering discipline to the slaves, tying his hands so that the supervisor could no longer practice physical punishment. I must confess that I, a slave, lost respect for my master.

By now I had been given full responsibility for the stewardship of Philemon's goods in his warehouses, for old Spyridus had been retired to freedom from slavery and given his papers of manumission. Even Philemon himself granted that I was very young for such a great responsibility. However, he put his trust in me. I believe Philemon would have been more careful had he not been lost in contemplation of his new faith.

Instead of carrying out the trust imposed on me, I reacted adversely. I thought that no one cared what I did. Consequently I became less and less interested in my work, and more concerned with pleasure for myself. And because this was possible for me, my contempt for Philemon grew apace.

Because the four or five years that passed after the departure of Epaphras from Colossae brought no great events, I must describe in brief the changes that took place. What happened to Philemon, to Archippus, to the Christian church of the city, and to me, left not one of us the same as we had been before.

While Philemon was reputedly the leader of the Christian church in Colossae, there were others who aspired to have their say. Those of the faith of Mithra who had listened to Epaphras, in his absence thought back again to the rituals of the grottoes. They missed the oriental devotions, the tapestry of legend and idolatry on which they had been nourished. Christianity lacked the holy stone tablets, the mystic fire, and the blood ceremonies. Why not some compromise, they urged. Surely the centuries-old cult of Mithra could not have been entirely wrong?

The priests of the synagogue had their opinions, too. Gentiles could not truly be Christians without circumcision and observance of the Hebraic law, they claimed. To circumvent the ritual of circumcision was fooling Gentiles into any easy conversion, the priests said. Was not Christ himself a Jew? They declared that the false doctrines circulated by Paul were a dangerous and unwarranted theology. To Colossians accustomed to long initiation ceremonials, such as the seven steps of Mithraism, the arguments of the Jews made sense.

Slowly then the practice of Christianity slipped from the precepts of Paul and Epaphras. Faith became diffused, obscured. And with the confusion in people's minds came doubts and the renewed worshiping of the old gods.

Even Philemon was affected. He became less sure of himself when the clear, urgent words of Paul that he had heard in Ephesus dimmed in memory. As I look back now, I can see that Philemon's difficulty lay in the first place in never having been converted to Christianity for Christ's sake. He had been influenced still by Persilio's death and his disappointment in the God of Light.

My master forfeited his leadership of the congregation in all but name. He began to lose his place in the community and his business declined.

Then Archippus did the most surprising thing. I have not before mentioned that he had become a fervent follower of Christ, perhaps the most sincere of all in Colossae. He had absorbed with eagerness all which Epaphras had taught. Now, when he saw the wayward action of the church in Colossae, he was deeply angered. He stormed at the elders for deviation. To emphasize his viewpoint, he declared himself a minister to Christ and renounced his previous way of living. He put on a haircloth robe and retired to a small room in a corner of Philemon's villa. From that time on he lived abstemiously and fasted often. He came forth only to preach on behalf of the ascetic life and to castigate the Colossians for their ways of ease.

Archippus found followers in self-denial among the young men of the town, who agreed with him to abandon normal lives of marriage and families and to adopt an existence of rigorous hardships.

All of this I could watch with a certain amusement, and I went my way without interference. My chief concern came to be the pursuit and fulfillment of day-to-day pleasure for myself. I did as little work as possible and took to spending much time on the streets of the town. I devoted myself to wine and loud company at meeting places of others like myself. It was not hard for me to divert money from Philemon's resources for my own purposes. I accounted in Philemon's trade to no one. The brothels of Colossae came to know me as a steady customer.

The lack of morale pervaded the servants' quarters, too. The slaves grumbled and quarreled, and licentiousness sprang up in the villa itself. Since Zalgrebbo had been restrained from physical punishment, he had abandoned all pretense of discipline.

I suppose that the only one to regret the decline in Philemon's household was Apphia. She sorrowed greatly, but was unable to bring her loved husband to his normal senses. I avoided meeting her. I could not find it in my heart to look into her grieving eyes.

Do I dare to make an apology for my own behavior? It is scarcely possible, but I do advance one extenuating circumstance in my own behalf. In the months and years after Ephesus, I was driven to distraction by the continuing memory of Aurelia. To love so briefly and so hopelessly should not shape the subsequent actions of any man. Yet I kept seeing her in my mind, and always I wondered what had befallen her. She could have been in the arms of one man after another, and I was jealous to the point of madness. This jealousy helped to drive me to the brothels of Colossae, and in each woman I tried to lose a little more of my memory of Aurelia.

This was the state of things when we received word that the trader Vergilio Pontius of Rome was traveling to Colossae.

The news shook Philemon into some action, for Vergilio wrote that he wanted to buy a quantity of fine black wool for the Roman market. Our own warehouse inventory was low. My master sent me on horseback into the countryside and down to Laodicea to make contracts for as many purchases as possible.

I succeeded in my search, although my mind had never been less on my work. That Vergilio should be coming to Colossae brought to me a desperate hope. Perhaps Aurelia would be with him. If so, I would renounce my evil ways forever. I dreamed. I allowed myself to plan on asking Philemon to buy Aurelia. Then we could be married and serve our master faithfully.

My hope grew, and with it a fear that Aurelia might

not accompany the Roman. I lived in a state of torment until the day arrived when Vergilio's small caravan reached Colossae.

We had sent a messenger to urge him to stay at Philemon's villa. I remember my anticipation when I ran out to the courtyard after hearing news of the visitor's arrival. Yes, he had a girl traveling with him as before. But not Aurelia. This girl was yellow-haired, large, with a pouting mouth. She was on the back of a camel, and her face was caked with the dust of the journey.

"Take me down from here," she cried to one of the drivers. "I have had more than enough."

"You have said more than enough!" Vergilio spoke sharply from his own camel. "Be quiet!"

Philemon came to welcome his guest and to escort him into the villa. Vergilio remembered me with a pleasant nod. Aeneas had stayed in Rome this time, he told my master. I wanted so to ask about Aurelia, but of course I could not then.

I saw to it that the servants, including the new girl, were taken to their quarters. Her glance at me was quizzical, as if to ask who I was. I gave her no reply. I was too disappointed.

Later in the day I came upon her in the garden. She was singing a song, accompanying herself on a lyre. Her voice was not as sweet or as pleasant as I remembered Aurelia's. But it was bolder, and she stopped when I passed near her.

"I practice a song for the entertainment tonight," she said. "You do not mind?"

"Certainly not," I said. "I was going to ask if your room is comfortable for you."

"I do not like my room," she said. "It is too far away from others in the house."

"I am sorry," I said. "It is in the section reserved for slaves."

I spoke with intentional scorn. I did not like this girl who had taken the place of Aurelia.

Her eyes grew narrow. "You are a slave yourself," she said.

My reply was worse than a small boy's retort. "Yes, but with a privileged status."

"No more privileged than I am. That is why I do not like my room."

"I know the work you do. I know you train for the life of the hetaerae. Vergilio purchased you from people in Rome who brought you up from childhood. When you are older, he will sell you for a good profit. Vergilio is a trader."

I could not explain why I spoke so to her, except that it relaxed some of the bitterness in my heart.

Now her eyes became wide. "How do you know all this?"

"I know everything except your name."

"I am called Gulda." She paused, then said, "You are holding something in my disfavor. Why?"

I retreated. "Oh, no! Until now I have not spoken with you. What should I hold?"

Her mouth pouted. "There is something."

"Yes," I said then. "What do you know of the girl Aurelia, who once was a slave to Vergilio?"

"So that is it," she said. She looked at me for a long time. "I understand she was sold to a certain senator in Rome. The sale was in secret, and his name was not revealed."

I felt sick in the pit of my stomach. "Ah. . . ." I said involuntarily.

"But there is a rumor," Gulda added softly, "that she was afterward presented to Octavia, wife of Nero, as a serving girl."

"To the wife of Nero!" I exclaimed. "And then. . . ."

"Who can say? Perhaps the rumor was wrong."

I drew in a very deep breath.

"I am glad to know," I told her. "And—I hold nothing against you."

I began to move away.

"One moment," she called. "I am also glad to know about you. I will keep the room in which I have been placed. You may come there tonight, if you wish, after the entertainment of the evening."

I glanced back at her. She was full in body and strong. "Perhaps," I said.

I did not go—not that night or any night during the time Vergilio stayed as guest in my master's villa. I had no further conversation with Gulda, except for an exchange of greeting when we met in the house.

At least, I could imagine Aurelia serving Octavia, wife of the Caesar. Only the best fortune could bring such a blessing to occur for her. But once closed inside the doors of the Imperial Palace, no power but that of Caesar himself could release Aurelia again.

What connection there may have been between Vergilio's visit and Philemon's next move I do not know. I suppose the shortage of goods to trade became all too apparent. Shortly after the Roman trader left Colossae, my master called me to his room.

Archippus was present, too. He appeared incongruous, as he spoke of business matters, in his long hairshirt.

Philemon reclined on his couch while Archippus restlessly paced the floor.

"Onesimus," my master began. He had regained some of the old black fire in his eyes now, and it was evident that he was very angry. "I have much that must be said to you."

"Yes, master."

"You have given me great displeasure."

I bowed my head. "I am not worthy to displease my master."

"You are named Onesimus, the useful one." Philemon rose from the couch. "I placed you in positions of trust despite your youth. I have placed dependence upon you, without calling for accountings."

Archippus interrupted, muttering, "Oh, useless one, from the beginning of the very beginning."

"You have betrayed my trust!" Philemon said.

"Yes, master," I whispered.

"I have been asleep in my confidence of you. But I have awakened. With Archippus to aid me, I have read over the inventory lists and the books of account. We have asked questions of others about you."

"Yes, master."

"You have failed in your keeping of my accounts; you have apportioned to yourself money not yours; you have taken to much wine and loud company; you have gone whoring!" Philemon was angrier than he had been for a long time. "You have set at nought the essence of loyalty throughout my household!"

"Indeed, master," I admitted.

"So much more, you have driven from my heart the gentleness of Christian spirit which I have made to govern my life." He shook his fist. "You have revived a long-dead spirit of evil within me."

"I am sorry, master."

"You have rejected, even scorned, baptism in Christ through which you could have redeemed your soul from sin!"

"You have blasphemed God and the church," Archippus added.

I looked down at the floor without replying.

"I must tell you that Archippus counsels me to dispose of you on the slave market," Philemon said.

"You have become a corrupting sore in our household," Archippus shouted at me. "We must cleanse ourselves of your presence."

I was made speechless by the violence of their condemnation. Immediately the full dishonor of my acts

struck into my heart. Once I had wished to love Philemon as I might have loved a father. Now I saw myself
as my master saw me, a despicable traitor to his trust.

But I could not stand the prospect of being sold in
disgrace on the slave market.

"Master, I was blind," I said abjectly. "Now I see. I
ask forgiveness."

"In accordance with precepts of the Christian faith, I
might have been constrained to show forgiveness," Philemon said. "I will not sell you. Yet I have lost so much
charity that I am ordering Zalgrebbo to give you lashes,
four times ten, in the presence of all males in this
household."

"Master!" I cried aghast.

"There is more." Philemon raised his hand. "I will
blame myself for not heretofore considering your age. I
have overlooked the fact that before now you should
have taken a wife."

"A wife, master!"

"Three women of our household are available for
marriage. They are the ones called Claudia, and Flavia,
and Julia. You will take one of them to yourself. See
that you discuss this matter with these three women,
and between yourselves decide promptly."

Archippus gave an alternative. "That is, unless you
abandon evil and follow a Christian life of celibacy as I
do," he added sharply.

I glanced from him to Philemon. Here indeed was an
ultimatum. Of the girls mentioned, Claudia was sharp-
tongued, and Julia was old and fat. Flavia, the most desirable, had turned Christian. I wanted none of them as
a companion in love. Yet Archippus' suggestion of the
hairshirt and self-denial suited me not at all.

"I will decide which course promptly, master, and
advise you."

Philemon nodded. His expression had grown even
darker. "I myself will attend the flogging by Zalgrebbo,"

he said. "That the servants of this household may know on which side they must stand! Now go. . . ."

I cannot tell whether the idea for my great defection came to me immediately after my upbraiding by Philemon and Archippus, or during the frightful and painful ordeal of the punishment by Zalgrebbo.

For this punishment I was stripped naked and lifted by chained wrists to a position where my toes scarcely touched the floor. The forty lashes were administered with a whip studded with chips of iron.

I believe I lost consciousness before the whipping was finished. I know only that I was tossed bleeding onto a pile of straw afterward, and left alone to recover. I had lost my privileged status, and I was a butt of shame before the household.

Even among the women, the only sympathy came from the Christian, Flavia, whom I despised for her faith. She cleaned the wounds of my body, and fed me, and cared for me during a full week of recovery.

After that, Zalgrebbo's functions and honors were reinstated. The morale of the household tightened again. I had been the unwilling agent of a revival of Philemon's former spirit.

But within myself bitterness turned to hatred, resentment changed to active revolt.

VII

I decided that I would run away from Philemon.

The consequences of such a crime I knew very well. To believe that because I was young I did not know what a terrible thing I contemplated would be false. No slave was unaware of the horrible results of being caught after running away.

Asian custom held slaves to the strictest standards of bondage. The Roman laws which prevailed in these provinces were interpreted harshly. Punishment for a runaway servant caught and returned to his master could be the grimmest torture, physical mutilation, and probable death. Or a master could transfer the culprit to the Roman governor for consignment to the games of the arena.

But even if not caught, a fugitive slave fared worse than a fleeing animal, for under severest penalties of law no hand could be raised in help or protection.

Yet I determined on my course. Torture and death seemed preferable to remaining under slavery. To escape from Philemon's servitude became an obsession. I craved freedom and the chance for wealth and pleasure of my own. After my flogging I came to hate my master, and Archippus who would in turn one day become master.

The prospect of marriage to one of the household women represented a final hell of bondage. I speak of marriage advisedly. The laws of marriage were written for all the population except slaves. Inasmuch as slaves were considered not as human beings but as chattels or things, the laws did not apply to them. Without the recognition of law, there could be no real marriage for slaves but merely a living together, which an owner could dignify with the name marriage if he chose. The level of indignity was about equal to the breeding of horses in the stable, even if in certain households like Philemon's unions were enforced by orders to be faithful on pain of punishment.

I would not yield to such a future.

Not least, I dreamed of Aurelia. Even if she were as

much beyond my reach as the limits of the sky, I could still be near her. I would go to Rome.

Using the best talents of my education and intelligence, I laid out a plan. The opportunities of my work greatly aided me.

To divert money for traveling from Philemon's reserves would have aroused suspicion at once, as my master now carefully watched my accounting. Yet I had access to the strongboxes of jewels in the stock of goods for trade. I could take a quantity of oriental gems including rubies, emeralds and sapphires without fear of immediate detection. The loss would not be discovered for quite a long time due to changes I made in the inventory lists. I filled a small cloth bag with jewels and sewed others into the lining of a new mantle which I purchased and kept hidden from sight.

As a document of identification I prepared a fictitious letter addressed to myself from one ostensibly my father, written as from Antioch. I had such a high quality of penmanship from Demetris' teaching that I could easily change from one style of writing to another without detection. In the letter, my imagined father requested me to proceed to Rome and learn there as much of commerce as would benefit a young man intending to follow his father's profession of merchant. I remember that I used the words, *Prepare yourself to be the same kind of loyal and useful citizen of the Roman Empire that I take pride in calling myself, and which our ancestors called themselves before us.* I signed the letter with a fictitious name—Julius Dorius, to give it a Roman flavor—and sealed the signature with an antique and valueless oriental seal I found in a box of worthless souvenirs. Further, from Philemon's file of business letters, I placed together documents that gave evidence of being special, signed introductions and references.

At one time the Roman governor at Laodicea had given Philemon a pass to permit his entry for trading purposes into an encampment of Roman legions. The pass had long been buried in old records and forgotten. However, I knew its location and took it. With great care I scratched out the name of Philemon and wrote in substitution a name which I selected for myself. It was Epaphras. What caused me to use the name of the Christian I cannot say. I enjoyed the sound of it, and I was convinced that I would never see the real Epaphras again. It seemed a name unlikely to cause me embarrassment, so I adopted it and added "Dorius" after it.

Thus I had a packet of identification documents—documents that would be sufficiently impressive even under more than a casual examination.

Chance favored me too. At about this time my master instructed me to proceed to Laodicea, some hour's ride down the river Lycus, for the collection of certain accounts, especially one of considerable size. Out of the proceeds I was to make settlement for the wool we had purchased for Vergilio. Philemon directed me to proceed to the neighboring town, perform this business, and return directly with the substantial balance of money left over. He would stand for no mischief, he said. Also, he informed me, he was becoming impatient over the delay in my decision about a woman of the household.

I reviewed my plans again very carefully, that there should be no error. I departed from Philemon's villa early one morning, without ceremony. I regretted leaving without the salutations of Apphia, but this benefit was clearly impossible. I took one of the best horses for the trip, a mount known for speed and endurance. I carried a short sword, and a quantity of dried dates and figs. I had also a piece of clean linen reserved for a special purpose. The new mantle, into the hem of which I had sewn the jewels, I rolled into a tight package so that it would not be noticed. However, over my shoulders I wore ostentatiously an old mantle well known by sight to belong to me.

I took care to secure my packet of identity records and the bag of jewels to a girdle belt around my waist under the tunic.

The road to Laodicea was reputed to be plagued by the marauders so common everywhere. My plans included this fact. I urged my horse down the road past the great gorges of the Lycus and through the wild rocky hills. By the time I arrived at Laodicea, I had made certain that my steed was heaving and foam-streaked.

At my first place of business I hurried into the house wild-eyed, stammering about thieves on horseback who had dashed down upon me and from whom I had escaped with the greatest difficulty. I pointed to my exhausted horse for proof. Again and again in Laodicea I repeated the story—until it was placed throughout the town.

I completed the business assigned before the noon hour, and I found to my expected satisfaction that the balance of money remaining in my hands was more than sufficient to carry me to Rome. I sat about preparations for my ostensible return to Colossae, laughing at offers of escort. So carefully were my plans laid that my start coincided with the siesta time when traffic on the road between the cities would be at a standstill.

With increasing excitement I rode on until I found the location I wanted. The place was deserted in all directions. I reined in my horse and dismounted. With my sword I made a wound on my forearm. As blood poured out I allowed it to flow onto the old mantle which must be recognized as being mine. When it was sufficiently blotted with dark red I dropped it to the ground and used the piece of clean linen to bind my wound. The sword I let fall on the sand as if it had dropped from a lifeless hand.

Quickly remounting, I rode my horse over the piece of clothing to trample it, and over and over the area with short twists and turns to give the appearance of a group of horses in a violent fight.

I then rode back and forth a dozen times to a nook behind a hill where a small group of horses could easily have hidden to waylay a chance traveler. I made considerable tracks also to the bank of the near-by river, where a body could have been dropped into the stream.

Having been so fortunate in this perfect carrying out of my plans, I returned to the road and sped swiftly along it for a little distance. Evidence of my ride was thoroughly lost among the wagon ruts and camel tracks. Making certain that no one had yet appeared to see me, I left the road where the ground was rocky and showed little mark of the horse's hoofs. I took a course away from the river and back into hilly country where sheep might graze but where people seldom went.

Here, on the side of a small hill, I dismounted. My heart beat rapidly and I was breathless, but more with excitement than with exhaustion. My horse needed rest for the journey ahead. I had used it hard through that day.

I took this pause to contemplate in my mind this act of mine. Had I made any mistake, any chance slip that might give me away? There was still time to return. No, my simulated murder or abduction by brigands by my own best judgment was flawless in detail, even to the disappearance of the money from Laodicea. It would serve to throw dust in the eyes of Philemon and Archippus until they discovered that the jewels were missing and that the inventory lists were falsely weighted. I was convinced that weeks would pass before these facts could be found out. By then the last traces of my escape would have vanished. Possibly even the discovery of my theft would not change belief in my murder.

The danger ahead lay in accidental detection, or in

suspicion which my forged papers might not allay. Only caution and a bold front could carry me past such risks.

Resting on the hillside, I took time to question myself on my action. Why had I run away from Philemon? I was a young man, still in my twenty-first year. I gambled security, life itself, against a haunted existence of fear and guilt for all of my remaining time. I could make many excuses, but in those moments when I doubted even myself, then and later, I am not certain that any excuse justified the terror in my heart.

Strangely enough, at this present time of my life as I set down my story with the greater wisdom I have acquired, I understand more clearly why I ran away from slavery under Philemon. I had lost faith in everything but freedom. No longer did I have religious faith, or faith in loyalty or other ideals. My faith in Philemon as father and master was gone. Faith in love, as for Aurelia, had been frustrated.

I was driven by some ancient instinct of mankind to escape from the bondage of my condition of life, physically and in spirit. I was urged on instinctively by man's search for self-dignity. Without knowing what freedom really meant, I accepted it in faith, in the terms of Epaphras who had said to me: "The substance of faith lies beyond human reasoning."

Looking back now with the accumulation of experience, I cannot blame that young man who then was I for his flight. On the contrary, I would do the same again.

I waited until the heat from the sun had cooled and then rode on. I avoided the shacks of shepherds, and kept out of the way of the caravan tracks which led in the direction of Ephesus. I skirted through the hills with the greatest care, watching for those real-life bands of marauders who would have re-enacted my masquerade of tragedy with the utmost reality. Always I kept in my sense of direction the route of the Ephesus road so that I would not lose myself among the trackless, barren hills.

Through the early hours of the night and later I rode by starlight, and I paused only long enough for a brief rest before dawn. My horse was strong, and I pushed along at its best pace. Shortly after daylight we paused again, the horse and I, hidden in a crevasse between boulders where the sun did not reach, and where we found a spring in the ground. I had already consumed some of the dried figs and dates, and now I ate more. I slept long.

By early afternoon I rode on again at a fast clip. The land became flatter and more cultivated, and I could guess that I was approaching Ephesus. Now I moved more carefully as the various caravan tracks from different parts of Asia converged. I did not wish to be seen yet.

At length I could look down from a hill to the distant sea. There was the rooftop of the great temple of Artemis near the city. Below was the dark river Caÿster that flowed out of the hills to the Aegean.

I had one more difficulty to surmount. My horse which belonged to Philemon had fulfilled its use. I dared not ride into Ephesus to sell it there, for horses were valuable and scarce enough to attract attention. A person such as I with my manner of dress would not be likely to own more than a pony at best. If I turned the animal loose, anyone finding it would wonder from whence it had come. The discovery might be reported to the authorities. A Roman centurion would find the matter interesting. Ownership of a horse could be traced. And if I killed the horse and left the carcass on the hillside, the mystery upon its discovery could be even greater.

Once more I was fortunate. Looking down from the

hill to the river, I saw an encampment of tents along the bank. People moved about, and horses were hobbled nearby. From the tents and from the manner of their dress, I guessed that these were desert nomads, probably come to Ephesus for supplies and trading.

A new plan came quickly to mind. I waited until shortly before twilight. Then I boldly rode down the hill, and walked the horse deliberately past the encampment. I made a show of nodding greeting to those who noticed me, so that in a few moments men, women and children poured from the tents to watch. Their eyes were not for me but for the horse, a far superior animal to the ones they possessed.

At a short distance below the tents, toward Ephesus and close to the river bank, I pretended to make my own camp. I hobbled the horse and laid out my remaining food supplies. Then, in the twilight, I walked ostentatiously into a grove of trees beside the river. From this shelter I turned to watch.

As I expected, in a few minutes two men appeared at my supposed encampment. They paused there and examined the horse. Stealthily they followed me, looking down at my footprints in the sand. By the last light I saw that both carried swords.

The time had come. I took my packet of identification documents in my hand. Then I went to the bank of the river and waded in through the reeds. I walked into the current chest deep, holding up the packet to keep it dry. Quietly I moved downstream, carefully making no ripples. There I waited, hidden by darkness and long grass.

Soon I heard the men fumbling along the shore. There was silence, and then more fumbling. In the darkness it was obvious that they were puzzled by my disappearance.

They did not question the situation too far. After a long silence I heard the sudden sound of galloping hoofbeats. The sound went off, not in the direction of the camp, but up the hill from whence I had come in the first place.

They had stolen the horse, as I had thought they would. They would make no reports to the authorities. Not Philemon, nor a Roman centurion, nor anyone outside of the desert tribesmen would ever hear of that steed again.

I waited longer, and suddenly a small object floated down the current near me. I reached out cautiously. It was one of my dried figs which had been thrown into the river. The nomads were at least doing their best to erase all trace of me.

I laughed to myself, and ate the fig. Then, very cautiously and quietly, I waded down the river for a long stretch at the same depth. When I was altogether certain of my safety, I came ashore.

Taking advantage of the darkness, I walked toward Ephesus until I had passed the temple of Artemis. I found a vineyard safely removed from the vicinity of houses. There, between two rows of vines, I disrobed and spread my wet clothing on the earth. Unclad, I slept through the warm night.

The morning sun quickly dried my tunic and mantle. Dressing again, and making myself as presentable as conditions permitted, I passed among groups of people proceeding toward the temple. With them, I entered the place of worship of the goddess Diana.

My situation was much changed since my earlier visit years before.

I rested for a time, and then left. As I went out of the temple, I placed a coin at the offering to appease the goddess—in case she did exist.

By discreet inquiries along the Ephesus waterfront, I discovered that a ship was to sail that afternoon for

Corinth. I paid for my passage and completed my arrangements.

At the time of the setting sun, the shoreline of Asia was dropping swiftly astern, and I had started on my journey.

VIII

I approached Rome on foot, the less to attract attention.

From Puteoli, the seaport far to the south, I had traveled up the Appian Road. I had been glad at last to leave the sea, for the journey from Ephesus was long and filled with fear of discovery. Three times on the way I changed vessels, the better to conceal the path of my flight. Thoroughness seemed wiser than haste. From Puteoli to Rome I was still as careful, each day taking a different conveyance. Usually it was some four-wheeled wagon carrying goods to the capital, with a driver anxious for company. Sometimes I found only a countryman's cart, and once I dared travel in the fast-moving chariot of a Roman citizen agreeable enough to share his vehicle. At night I slept in fields or asked shelter in farmhouses, avoiding inns which might be nests of dangerous gossip as well as robbery and murder.

Each day I told the story that I was from Antioch, the son of a merchant, and that I traveled to gain experience and to enjoy the world before settling into my father's business.

No one questioned me, or asked to see my identity papers.

My money and the precious store of jewels I kept divided, some secured in the girdle pouch under my tunic and the rest still sewed carefully into the seams of my mantle.

At last, riding on a teamster's wagon, I reached the crest of the Alban Hills. My spirits soared. I was a youth eager and strong; and here was Rome, capital of the Empire, hub of the world. This was the city of which I had dreamed, where I would lose the past of servitude and start anew. Here lay the opportunities for which I had hoped so long. Here, I trusted, Aurelia still lived. Should one blame me that my heart leapt up as I looked down the arrow-straight Appian Road into the core of Rome?

I remained with the teamster's wagon until we reached a crossroads in the valley. There I left the driver, saying that I was bound for Ostia and the sea. But instead of turning left at the crossroads for Ostia, I walked straight on while the busy traffic of the Appian Road flowed by me in both directions. I saw the temples built along the route, and the tombs and the great arched grandeur of the viaducts. My fear of attracting attention here was unnecessary. No one turned a head or cast a glance at a young man in a commonplace mantle, carrying a sack of belongings and striding over the cobbled paving.

Then before me appeared the walls of Rome, high and formidable. The road led into the city by the Porta Appia, and I had to walk cautiously through the confusion of carts and chariots and litters which moved under the gate. Suddenly I was in Rome.

Nothing in Colossae or Ephesus or the cities along the way had prepared me for such numbers of people, such multitude of handcarts, bearers of boxes and baskets, horseback riders. For a moment I sought the shelter of a protecting wall. The city overpowered me. I was to learn later that wagons were forbidden to move on the streets of Rome during daylight. Even so, the flow of people engulfed the stranger.

I followed the crowds along the street, and I nearly lost my breath when I saw all at one time the famous Circus Maximus and, on the hill above, the magnificent façades of the Imperial Palaces of the Palatine. In that one amazing panorama the splendor of Rome made itself manifest to every new arrival on entry, just as Augustus years before had planned. I paused long enough to speculate on the length and circumference of the huge stadium, and to wonder which of the great palaces had belonged to what Caesar. I was stunned by this magnificence—a grandeur that even old Demetris, my teacher, in his most extravagant language had been unable to describe.

In one of those fantastic palaces—I could not even guess which one—Aurelia might be hidden away. With this possibility of her being so near, she was more remote than ever. Those imposing walls left no possibility of illusion about tracing one slave serving girl.

And the rumor, after all, might never have been true, and perhaps she of whom I had dreamed so long was the mistress of a senator, or by now lost forever among the prostitutes of the Roman brothels. Time moved quickly for those of her profession.

I walked along slowly, gazing at the Roman people— the tradesmen, artisans, soldiers, citizens in purple-bordered togas, slaves, perfumed youths and women. I was accustomed to seeing housewives at their marketing in public streets, but that women of the privileged classes were carried about abroad in uncurtained litters astonished me. Heedless of rude and curious glances they stretched themselves languidly in their conveyances, often not even covering their sandaled feet with a robe. They greeted friends with casual waves, or talked to men who trotted beside them like dogs under a leash.

Beyond the Palatine, I came to the Via Sacra leading to the Roman Forum in the valley between the Palatine and Capitoline hills. I saw the temples and shrines, and stood before the sanctuaries of the gods who were presumed to guide the destinies of the Empire.

The glory of the temples of Saturn, of Vesta, of Apollo and Venus, and the temples to the deified Caesars, Julius and Augustus—like that temple of Artemis in Ephesus—seemed to prove the greatness of the gods. Could it be possible, I wondered, that all this grandeur of marble and stone and bronze on earth was not equaled also in some Olympian place?

Mithra, I thought, had never made such a show as this. Nor had the God of the Jews, nor the one they called his Son, Jesus Christ. I had heard of no Caesars bowing down to them.

My irreligious contempt of the Roman gods was shaken on that first day in the city. I had to ask myself whether they were not, after all, true gods? Did they exist, as I had been told they did not? The Caesars believed they did. Who was I, and who were the other doubters, to question the faith of the Caesars?

When I stood before the temple of Vesta, most sacred in Rome, I paused even longer. How much I had heard of this sanctum where the holy fires had burned through long centuries! I was frightened by the majesty of the shrine which contained the mysteries of the Vestals. I remembered the story that Aurelia had told of the virgin who broke her vows of chastity, and of how Aurelia said that she cried through the night in sympathy with the girl so frightfully punished.

Was it strange that Aurelia, the slave, the hetaera, the concubine, should cry for a girl who sacrificed life for the loss of virginity?

As I gaped at the temples, I became aware of the attention of a curious Praetorian Guard. He was studying me carefully. He wore a helmet, and light armor over a short tunic. A sword hung at his side, while one hand rested on the hilt.

Suddenly I knew I was in danger. The search by the authorities for escaped slaves continued all the time, and I realized at once how obviously a stranger I was to Rome. All my actions indicated a recent arrival, despite my previous precautions. No one could have been acting more suspiciously.

Without glancing again at the guard I began to walk away in a brisk manner. I must never give an impression of idleness, I thought, or of being a stranger. I passed on through the Forum purposefully, scarcely glancing now to one side or the other.

I lost myself in the narrow streets of the city beyond the Capitol.

Rome then was in the seventh year of the rule of Nero, twenty-four years of age. Whatever may be said now of the Caesar, in that year people were satisfied. The young emperor was much given to pleasure, but in government he acceded to the wise guidance of his counselors, Seneca and Burrus. The war against the Parthians in Syria, north of Damascus, had gone well. Nearer at hand, an incipient revolt among Roman legions had been stamped out. Improvements were being made throughout the city of Rome. No one had much cause for complaint.

If any citizen thought it worth-while to speak openly of Nero's supposed murder of his mother, there were others to remind him quickly of Agrippina's own reputation for deadly intrigue. Was it not well known that Agrippina poisoned the Caesar Claudius, her third husband, in order to put Nero, her son by her first marriage, into power? Could anyone doubt Nero's claim that she had plotted in turn against him?

Other citizens deplored the Caesar's attention to his mistress Poppaea in the Imperial Palace, while his wife, the beautiful and popular Octavia, languished in her own apartments. But then, Nero was Caesar. The domestic affairs of Caesar were not the business of the people.

On the surface, Rome was quiet enough at the time when I, under the fictitious name of Epaphras Dorius, arrived there expecting to make a life of freedom and fortune.

I found a room which I could rent in a house near the great temple of the Pantheon. The room was on an upper floor, and the woman of the house was satisfied with my explanation of my presence in Rome. The house was in an alley off a small piazza, and it offered to me a good degree of anonymity.

Also I found employment to my satisfaction in the publishing house of Barea. The business of publishing flourished in Rome, with modern writing as well as the classics being in great demand. The public awaited with eagerness the latest essays, plays, and poems, and the Roman imperial library was a vast storehouse of literature. My education in languages, the arts, and philosophy was useful to the publisher, and the fine manner of handwriting which I had learned from my teacher Demetris proved valuable.

Every publisher maintained a large staff of slaves to carry on the copying of manuscripts. I was highly enough qualified to gain a special position above the slaves to carry out different kinds of duties at the publisher's discretion.

A part of my work was to transcribe letters dictated to me by clients of the publisher. I was sent out often to perform this service at the homes or places of business of the clients. Most of the letters referred to business subjects, and others to legal affairs. My experience in these matters made me of invaluable help.

Now, I had living quarters and an occupation with

reasonable remuneration. I could feel much more confident of hiding my real status. I dared hope that in time I could assume for myself the position of citizen, and start a business of my own.

These things accomplished, my greatest concern was to find out whether Aurelia really was a serving girl with Octavia, the wife of Nero, or whether she was lost in some dark backroom of the city. To know for certainty became my obsession.

IX

In time, it seemed desirable for me to begin the slow disposition of my jewels. I needed to make an investment in clothing, and also in books for my self-improvement. With money available, I would be able when it was feasible to set up my own contemplated business establishment—perhaps even to buy one or two slaves.

I waited until I had become more familiar with Rome, and its streets and markets. I discovered a small shop where a Spaniard by name of Yrujo did a special business with wealthy clients. Yrujo bought the jewelry of persons in urgent need of money; and he sold, too, at the lowest prices exquisite gems to those discreet enough not to ask him their origin. He was a ready buyer for whatever of value was no longer needed or wanted, and a convenient source for clandestine gifts. Citizens of Rome never questioned Yrujo's honesty. He was too useful to them.

I approached this Spaniard late one afternoon with a small handful of rubies and carved onyx. I included several larger sapphires, but my principal supply I retained.

The shop was dark. Yrujo examined carefully what I had. He looked at me with small eyes that shone above the lamplight turned onto the gem.

"Young man," he said, "these stones are exceptional. I am an honest dealer."

"My father in Antioch gave them to me to sell when I needed money," I told him. "One day I wish to buy my own business."

He examined the stones again. "These are rarely found on the market," he told me. "There is only one trader in Phrygia who has become well known for his supply of such gems."

I shrugged my shoulders, although my heart beat suddenly fast. "My father has had them a long time," I said. "I do not know how he obtained them."

The Spaniard smiled slyly. "You had best say he obtained them in Alexandria. That would be possible."

I could not answer. I hoped that I could trust this small-eyed, dark Spaniard into whose hands I had delivered myself.

He said, "I cannot buy these jewels from you. They are of high value, and I myself would be questioned seriously by the authorities on how I came to have them. What could I say? I told you that I am an honest man. I will act for you on the basis of a commission, and see what can be done."

I had little choice but to accept the arrangement, and therefore nodded. "I have a few more," I added.

"Of course you do." he said. "I know that you would not bring all to me on the first visit."

He gave me a receipt for those he retained as samples.

For the next several weeks I waited hopefully for Yrujo to take some action. Several times I stopped to peer into his dark shop. Each time the Spaniard shook his head.

"Give me time," he said.

I began to wonder whether I had selected a good man to handle my transactions. I was most impatient to obtain new clothes.

Each morning I reported for work at the publishing house of Barea, and my employer often sent me on assignments to transcribe letters. This business on the side, making use of his handwriting experts, was profitable to him. I myself enjoyed the assignments, for I could meet interesting people without great danger of detection. Also I was able to become familiar with the streets of the city and with the business and political life of the Empire.

One morning I was sent to an address on the Via Lata, opposite a well for drinking water. The name of the client meant nothing to me at the time—one Paul, the publisher said.

"The man is confined to his house as a civil prisoner," I was told. "I believe he awaits trial before the Emperor. Meanwhile, he writes many letters, and he is most exacting in his requirements. He has not been satisfied with those whom we sent in the past."

That the client was a prisoner should have been my first warning of danger. I should have understood that a house of confinement meant a guard, undoubtedly one of the Praetorian cohorts. But I was not alert enough to think of it.

I walked to the address given and found the house without difficulty. It was on a corner, where the Via Lata abuts against an ancient city wall now in disuse. I knocked on the door.

The answer was prompt. The man who responded was smooth-shaven, of medium age, with warm eyes and a pleasant smile. In fact, his face and his manner were so disarming that he gave an immediate impression of friendship. Although I knew I had not met this man before, he was disturbingly familiar to me.

"Good day," he said. "Enter please."

"I am the scribe sent by Barea," I explained.

"I assumed so," he said. "You have not been here before?"

"No. I was employed by Barea only recently."

He closed the door, and motioned to me. "You will come this way."

He led me through a large room to a door at the back. Here he in turn knocked.

"Master, it is I, Luke. The new writer of letters is here," he called through the door.

His face still troubled me. Without speaking to him, I was certain that I had seen this man before, as if he had perhaps been one who stood out in a crowd.

I had no further time for conjecture.

"Come, then," a voice replied from inside the room. "I am ready."

I could not fail to be struck by the tone of that voice. It was low, and yet it penetrated through the closed door as if no barrier had been there.

My guide pushed the door open and nodded to me. I followed him into the room.

It was small, with one narrow window opening onto the backyard of the house. The light fell mostly upon a table with manuscripts. Standing by the door, so that I brushed him in passing, was a soldier of the Praetorian Guard.

I trembled in sudden terror, but the soldier looked at me only casually. I had time for no more than the briefest glance at him.

A man sat on a couch at one side of the room. He had a massive beard, but most of the hair on the top of his head was gone. He was not a large man, but at once one felt the tremendous strength of his nature. He too was familiar. . . .

I remembered. The disturbance in Ephesus—Paul, the Christian, the man who dared to defy the crowd!

Now I recognized the other one also. He had been the man with the benevolent face who with Epaphras had restrained Paul from facing the mob.

"Master, the letter writer from Barea," my guide said, introducing me. He said to me, "You will transcribe for Paul, of Tarsus."

I stared at them both, from one to the other. My feelings spun in the astonishment and the fear which had seized me.

Paul leaned forward. "I believe the young man from Barea is speechless," he said drily. "Perhaps his pen is more communicative than his tongue."

"Pardon, pardon," I gasped. "I will transcribe. . . ."

I was still acutely aware of the soldier behind me. It was the most uncomfortable situation.

"And by what name are you called?" Paul asked.

"Onesimus," I replied.

Immediately I choked at hearing the sound of my own voice speaking the word I should never have uttered again. It was too late to recall it. I stood with fingers twitching.

"The one who is useful," Paul said. "I hope one more so than those who have come here before. We will go about the business at hand. You have your pen?"

"Yes, master," I replied.

The man named Luke withdrew after an encouraging nod. I was relieved to see the soldier follow him. The door closed, and I was alone with Paul, the Christian.

I cannot say now what letters I wrote for Paul on that first day, or what words I put down as he spoke them. At first I was nervous, and spoiled the sheet of papyrus with ink. I was clumsy, too, with the reed pen, as my fingers had the strength of nothing; but he was considerate to me and gave me an opportunity to correct the work.

As I remembered the fury of this man on that day in Ephesus, so I was astonished that he could be so gentle. He spoke softly, and there was love in his voice. His strength was not alone in the muscles of his arms, but in his tone, in his manner, in his thoughts. He was gentle in the very way in which he walked across the floor while he dictated his letters; but strength was always there, a strength of nature so powerful that as a man he was like no other.

These were the thoughts which I had that day, while the fear that I would betray myself further wore off. At last, however unwillingly, I was under a spell wrought by Paul of Tarsus. The spell was not of magic. It lay in the complete possession that he took of one's spirit.

I sat on a stool at the little table by the window, and found that I was not stirring except for the motion of my hand, writing. I held my breath to wait for the sound of his voice, speaking slowly, distinctly, and thoughtfully. He was a deep and careful thinker, and his letters were to friends—I remember as much as that— in Jerusalem, Athens, Corinth. His subjects were related to the Christian faith.

It became clear to me before long why Paul was a leader of the new sect which believed Christ to be the Messiah for all mankind. He was more than a leader. Because of his wisdom and judgment, he was a key to the whole, a rock on which the structure of the new faith was being erected. Yet, from his dictated letters, I understood that he faced much opposition from both within and without the body of Christianity.

He never forgot the reason for the soldier outside the door. He was a man imprisoned, although I decided that he must be of great importance to be allowed the freedom of his own house. I do remember that in his letters he uttered expressions almost of joy at his confinement. His imprisonment for the sake of Christ had become known everywhere, he said, even throughout the Imperial Palace. He was certain that the gospel, of which I had heard Epaphras speak so much in Colossae, had been spread much further with the news of what had happened to him. Paul said that even though the end be death for him, he would rejoice.

That any man could look so calmly upon a condition of terrible danger astonished me. I could not then comprehend the meaning of such strength of spirit.

When he had finished his dictation, Paul read the letters I had transcribed. He was satisfied, and he commended me upon my skill of writing.

"Onesimus," he said, forcing me to look deep into his eyes, "I have tried long to find someone as useful. You will come again. I have much work to do."

"Yes, master."

All this while I had been planning never to return to the house where danger so obviously lurked.

"You can indeed be of help to me," he said, and his gaze seemed to pierce me. "Perhaps of more help than you would now believe."

"Yes, master."

He raised his hand. "And may the peace of God, which passes all understanding, be with you."

I fled from the room.

I could have shed tears, not so much of emotion for anything said or not said, but rather because I knew suddenly that there were many things I could not understand. I had been content with what I thought I knew. After the assignment to write letters for Paul, I lost that contentment.

Hastily I made for the front door of the house, quickly passing the soldier and hoping to avoid Luke. As I opened the door to leave, I met someone coming in.

It was Epaphras. We stared into each other's eyes.

To Epaphras, seeing me meant a bridging of years. I perceived that he was probing his memory for someone long forgotten out of a multitude of forgotten persons. It meant to him a swift return over long travels and distant cities, a review of the many churches he had founded.

To me, the sight of Epaphras meant the terror of doom, the end of all hopes and plans. The one terrible risk I had taken was that of recognition. But, I had thought, who in Rome would recognize me, or be familiar enough with me to connect a supposed recognition with the reality of my being in the city?

The only one I had even anticipated seeing was Aurelia, and to her I would willingly have entrusted my life if I had been able to find her.

But that Epaphras should be in Rome—and being there should meet me in a doorway face to face—I thought must be the act of an evil spirit. Yet this meeting was not strange at all when fully considered. Epaphras—like Luke, and like Timothy whom I had not heard of then—was one of Paul's close friends and assistants. Where one was, so were the others.

"Onesimus of Colossae!"

I waited for him to call the Praetorian Guard from within, to hear him say, *This man is a fugitive, a slave escaped from his master! Take him away!*

"But how far you are from home!" Epaphras cried. With eagerness he asked, "Is Philemon in Rome? Did you travel here with him?"

"No," I said in misery. "No, he is not in Rome. Philemon is in Colossae."

Epaphras looked at me with an increasingly odd expression. He hesitated. "Then he sent you here—on business? Or with a message for us, for Paul?"

Could I have lied? No lie was possible in answering that question.

"No . . . no, he did not send me."

After a moment he said, "I begin to understand. Let us not remain here in the doorway. Come in."

I stepped back into the house. "The guard?" I whispered.

Epaphras frowned. "I had not thought of that. We will go this way."

He opened another door, into a small room at the front of the house. I entered before him.

"I will ask you no questions," Epaphras said, "except one: You have become a Christian?"

"No!" I cried. "No, I was sent here on an assignment, to transcribe letters. It is my work."

I held up my pen for evidence.

"You are the same Onesimus," he said, laughing. "So it is only work that brings you to this house?"

"I did not know beforehand where I was going."

"You mean into the den of Christians? We are not likely to claw you apart."

"You will not tell the guard?"

"What lies between you and the guard is your affair, not mine."

"But the law. . . ."

Epaphras shrugged. "There is the law of God, and there is the law of man," he said. "It is necessary to believe in both in their respective ways; but I will not report you. I know nothing of you."

When the doomed are reprieved, light shines again with brightest colors. The feeling of life in the veins beats faster.

"Thank you, Epaphras," I said. "You take a great danger for me. I will not come here again."

"Why not?" he said. "It is the same to me." He laughed with a cheerfulness which I could not share. "And you must become a Christian yet, to find forgiveness in heaven for this sin!"

X

The Christian apostle commended my work to my employer Barea, and requested that I be sent back to him. I had little choice but to return to the house of Paul. To refuse would have meant difficult explanations.

The error I had made in giving my true name to Paul nearly brought disaster. I had not corrected the Christians, and they sent for me as the scribe, Onesimus.

"I do not understand this," Barea said to me. "I believe they refer to you, but you have given your name to me as Epaphras."

"It is a conceit of the Christian," I explained nervously. "He told me that I was *onesimus,* or useful to him. He has forgotten."

"Of course," the publisher said. "That would be it. I was puzzled at first."

In my daily life in Rome, I found myself becoming more and more furtive. The unceasing strain of existing under false identity bore down heavily. I took my meals in the house where I lived. I made no friends and seldom spoke to anyone. I walked on the streets with care that no one followed me. In all that I did, I stayed under persistent fear.

The illusion of freedom was more empty than I had ever imagined. I was not free at all.

When I went for the second time to the house of the Christians, this fear went with me. As I knocked this time, another man opened the door. I explained once again that I was the scribe sent by Barea.

"The one named Onesimus?" the stranger asked. "Indeed my friend Epaphras has told me of you."

"Epaphras did?" I said with faint voice.

"Yes, he told me that the master is much pleased by your penmanship. I am Tychicus, another of Paul's fellows in the Christian faith."

So it was that I met the one whom in time I would come to know so well—Tychicus of Asia, the companion of Paul and ardent disciple of Christianity. Although he was no longer young, he was smooth shaven and had dark hair that grew long. He was shrewd but likable, with the frankness and sincerity that characterized Paul's associates.

At that first meeting with Tychicus I was naturally doubtful of him. Yet he gave me no more cause to question his motives than Epaphras did. No one in that house ever asked questions concerning my origin or my purpose in Rome. By my accent and clothing, by my mannerisms and the fact that my name was of Greek source, they must have known that I was not native to Rome. But if they were curious, they never said so to me.

Tychicus led me back to the door of Paul's room. Everything was much the same as before. Paul sat in deep thought on the couch, and the soldier stood at the door. The apostle nodded as I entered. Without a word the guard moved out, and Tychicus left us alone again.

I took my place at the table by the window, with sheets and pen ready. Paul remained thinking, not moving or speaking. I had a long opportunity to observe him discreetly.

I had thought much concerning Paul since my first visit here. It had been impossible to put him out of my mind. The light in his eyes, the way he moved, and the depth of his voice were haunting things. The power of his character frightened me. I did not want to think about him or about any Christian. I had had enough of Christianity in Colossae.

I could not seem to escape from this religious faith centering on Jesus Christ. It had followed me from Ephesus to Colossae, and now to Rome. I was more contemptuous of it than ever, or at least I made myself believe so. If I were to acknowledge any religion now, I would follow the gods of the Romans, perhaps Vesta or Apollo. The grand solidity of their majestic temples in Rome were proof to me that, if there be gods, these held power eternal.

A god was a *god,* ruling in some unknown Olympus or celestial place. A god could not be a man. If Christ was a man, he could not be a god—so I reasoned to myself. Paul was not a god, for he, too, was a man. This argument was conclusive for me, until I remembered that the Roman emperors beginning with Julius Caesar were deified. Caesar and Augustus had been men, yet now they were called gods. Julius Caesar had claimed descent from the goddess Venus. If he was right, and Augustus and most Romans had believed that he was, then my reasoning about the humanity of Christ led nowhere.

I wished to put all religious matters once and forever from my mind. Looking at Paul deep in meditation that morning, it occurred to me that such negation was impossible. To repudiate all religious faith was not in the nature of man.

He looked up at last and said, "Now we will begin."

Certain words that Paul spoke for me to write down in the letter he dictated that morning I remember particularly: "Therefore, my beloved, as you have always obeyed, so now, not only as in my presence but much more in my absence, work out your own salvation with fear and trembling; for God is at work in you, both to will and to work for his good pleasure."

As I wrote the phrase, *work out your own salvation with fear and trembling,* I glanced at him. It was an inadvertent move on my part. The thought expressed seemed particularly relevant to me—that was all.

I caught Paul's steady gaze on me. He had remained sitting on the couch, watching me intently.

"Do you understand what you write?" he asked.

"No," I replied.

"I speak of a kind of fear and trembling different from what you think," he said. "I speak of fear of God. To fear God is to honor and respect his commandments. If a man fears God, he need fear no man."

I had no answer to make.

"You are afraid of man, Onesimus," he told me. "You think to work out your salvation in fear and trembling before man."

"But how else. . . ."

"Only through God does one find salvation."

I had to look back at the papyrus sheet before me.

"Do you understand now what you write?" he asked me again.

"I suppose so." My voice was a whisper. The truth was that I did not want to understand; I wanted to have no part of these Christian philosophies. I shut my ears to the arguments. Changing the subject, I said, "Will you repeat again what comes after?"

"For God is at work in you, both to will and to work for his good pleasure."

The words had been spoken to me, deliberately. They were meant to be personal words, whereby Paul told me plainly that God was within me, endeavoring to have me accept and follow his way. I did indeed feel sudden fear and trembling, in spite of myself, not of man but of the presence of this unknown God of whom Paul spoke.

I wrote the words into the letter.

That morning, after finishing my work, I started away from the house dazed and shaken. However I tried, I could not throw off Paul's influence. On my way to Barea, I met Epaphras again on the street.

"Will you stay with us today?" he asked. "You can share our noonday meal."

"No," I said hastily. "I must return to my employer. Thanks to you, nevertheless."

"Another time then. You could plan to stay."

I hesitated. "You do not know what you say," I told him. "You cannot safely give shelter to one in my position. The law. . . ."

Epaphras laughed. "In our house we have no fear," he said. "We will shelter any man. God will protect us."

I glanced at him. What Epaphras said seemed to put into practice the meaning of the words Paul had spoken to me, about fear of God and fear of man.

Then I had something to tell Epaphras, a most difficult thing to explain. I stumbled out with it.

"The name by which I am known in Rome, to Barea and others," I managed to say. "It is not Onesimus. The name I used on my documents—and to whomsoever I have had to give it—is Epaphras."

"Epaphras!"

"Epaphras Dorius, of Antioch, son of one Julius Dorius, merchant."

"Why Epaphras?"

"I never thought to see you here, or anywhere, again. I . . . I thought it a good name."

He recovered himself.

"I think it is, too," he said gravely. But his eyes twinkled. "When we send for you again, we shall send for Epaphras Dorius, the scribe."

"Thank you," I said, and ran from him.

I went again and again to the house of Paul on the Via Lata, so that my work there became a regular thing.

The house of Paul came to have a comforting effect on me. I soon found it to be the one place in Rome where I did not have the constant horror of being discovered for what I was. That the house of Paul's imprisonment, under constant watch of Praetorian soldiers, should seem safe to me was the strangest of paradoxes. Did the explanation lie in the sober peace of mind of its occupants?

Once I stayed for the noonday meal. I came to know Tychicus, and Luke who, I learned, was a physician. Also there was Timothy of Galatia, beyond Phrygia, who had long been with Paul. These three along with Epaphras, I could call friends.

Paul, I was told, had been imprisoned in Palestine and brought from there to Rome after his appeal to the Emperor. The charges against him were instigated by Hebrew priests, the opponents of that Christianity which had sprung out of their own synagogues. The charges, which I understood to be of incitement to civil commotion and disturbance, were vague enough to puzzle the Roman authorities. This lack of specific citation, as well as Paul's citizenship rank, persuaded the government to confine him merely to the house he had rented for himself.

The presence of the guard was the chief indication that Paul was under any kind of restraint. He could receive the numerous visitors who came to see him and to hear him carry on his ministry; he could perform his work and write letters. The dwelling on the Via Lata became the center for Christian effort not only in Rome, but by remote guidance throughout the Empire.

Still, the impact of Christianity failed to touch me deeply. I listened to Paul's dictated words and then wrote them down without absorbing them into myself.

I heard Luke, Epaphras, and Tychicus speaking earnestly of the gospel they had taught to hundreds of converts, and still I placed myself apart.

I turned my heart against faith in any form of god. I had before me the lesson learned in Colossae from Philemon, who had drowned himself first in the rituals of Mithraism and later in the spiritual sacrifices of Christianity.

My physical freedom was in jeopardy enough. I did not intend to lose myself in spiritual servitude.

XI

One day I knocked again at the door of Yrujo's shop, more in despair than hope. I had nearly given up the thought that anything would come of his efforts to sell my jewels, but with the approach of the cold and rain of winter, my need for clothing grew desperate.

To my relief, this time the Spaniard motioned to me to enter the dark front room of the shop.

"I have had a client," he told me. "There is money for you."

He took a small bag from a box and handed it to me. He made no attempt to explain the transaction or to account for the stones. I accepted the bag and found that it was heavy.

"Now," the Spaniard said, "you will bring a new selection of even better grade. There is one highly placed in the Imperial Palace who may have interest in your stones, but he demands the finest quality."

"I will bring the jewels." I paused. "You are acquainted with someone in the palace?"

"In my business," he said, "I am acquainted with everyone, and yet with no one."

It was a sudden opportunity that I saw then, the chance for which I had been waiting. To take it was bold and rash, but I did not hesitate.

"There may be a certain serving girl at the palace," I said as casually as I could. "I was asked to obtain news of her, if she be still alive. I should write to those who asked for her."

"The palace is large. There are many girls."

"She is rumored to be a slave girl to Octavia, wife of Caesar."

Yrujo's gaze did not reveal any trace of what he thought.

"Then it might be possible," he said cautiously. "The name of the girl?"

"Aurelia."

"Usually questions are not asked about the household of the Caesar. Yet it might be learned whether a certain girl named Aurelia is in the service of Octavia."

"My commission to you would be the higher," I said.

He smiled. "It may be possible," he repeated.

I took the new stones to him the following day, still retaining the best. Then I waited for the three days which he told me would pass before he had news. Never did time move so slowly. I curbed my anxiety, and on the third day returned to the shop.

"There *is* a girl Aurelia in the service of Octavia," Yrujo said. "Perhaps it is the one of whom you spoke."

I gasped. "It is true, then? Did you learn more?"

"You asked no more," the Spaniard said. "I have learned enough."

My certain knowledge that Aurelia lived in the Imperial Palace left me even more helpless than before. How could I approach her? She was as far from reach as ever.

But Yrujo was smiling slyly. "You might wish to offer your jewels to Octavia herself?" he said. "I understand that at times she is receptive to goods of special interest. Perhaps you could learn more of the one you seek."

"I!" I gasped. "I go to Octavia?"

"A guilty conscience is as great a liability as a stolen jewel," he told me. "You must learn to keep your conscience from revealing itself in your face."

"Oh," I said, without means of denial.

"You may carry this letter of introduction from me," he said. "The way is prepared. You will proceed to the palace of the Emperor, and ask to be taken before the wife of Caesar. This time show your best stones."

"Yes," I said. "I will not be questioned?"

"Why?" he asked. "Only be sure to remember your story as you have told it to me."

I took the letter from his hand.

"Thank you," I said.

The Spaniard did not mention the second set of jewels I had given him, or give me any further money. I was too excited to ask.

I went early in the evening under the first gold of the Roman twilight. It was a time, I hoped, when palace discipline would be at its lowest ebb. Nighttime revelries would be beginning, and little attention would be paid to a solitary individual approaching the Palatine.

On a belt hidden by my mantle I carried a bagful of choice stones from my jewel collection. In another sack were the valuable identity documents. The procedures of palaces and imperial customs were unfamiliar to me, and I had the disadvantage of being unable to ask advice. I could do no better than proceed to the main entrance of the palace with my head held high in false assurance.

The entry was alive with persons coming and going. All manner of distinguished citizens including senators walked side by side with the servant classes. I was not challenged at the gate, and I entered past the Praetorian Guard into an elaborate courtyard.

My greatest danger lay in hesitation. If I showed signs of doubt, the watchful guards would notice me at once and take me for questioning. The Spaniard's letter might be a sufficient passport, but I did not want a curious Praetorian lieutenant to probe more deeply into my story. So I walked through that courtyard as if I knew exactly where I was going. Meanwhile, I glanced quickly in every direction at once.

One entrance, judging by the number of people entering and leaving, clearly led to the main part of the palace. I saw more togas, worn only by Romans of rank, than I had ever thought could be in one place. A squad of soldiers was taking out a prisoner, a poor, almost inanimate creature in chains—being pushed and pulled along to a certain doom, probably in the arena. I allowed myself only the most casual glance in his direction. Except for caution, there would be I.

Perfumed women in litters were carried into the palace by slaves. Pedestrians usually moved deferentially out of their way. The women of the palace could be influential, and often a whispered word in the right or wrong ear meant all the difference in a man's career.

Here was the center of all the Empire's intrigue. Here all the nationalities of the Roman world were represented: business combines seeking favors, the wealthy hoping to increase their fortunes or at least to save them from the Emperor's clutch, and the poor begging for substance. For Caesar's word was the law, and none could say him no. Little the wonder that I trembled for the risk I took—not so much a risk of recognition by name but rather a risk of recognition of what I was. Although clean, my mantle was fraying at the hems. My sandals were old. I might well present to all these worldly people, I thought, the exact picture of a young slave escaped.

The quick examination that I made of the courtyard while I walked so purposefully through it showed other entries to the palace besides the chief one. In one corner a passageway, like a tunnel, appeared to lead in the general direction of the Palatine.

I saw an old man leaning idly against a wall, and I took the chance that he might help me. I went directly to him.

"Where may I find the wife of Caesar, Octavia?" I boldly asked.

He looked at me disdainfully. "You know little of Rome to think that you will find the wife of Caesar in Caesar's quarters. It has not been so from the beginning."

"I understand that, but where does she keep herself at this present time?"

The old man began to enjoy himself, to my discomfort.

"She does not keep herself there; the Caesar keeps her," he told me. "He keeps another where she should be."

He referred to Poppaea, Nero's mistress, who lived with the Emperor in the palace while Octavia remained elsewhere in seclusion.

The unsuccessful outcome of the marriage of Octavia and Nero was commonly known. Through the marriage long before of the then-Caesar Claudius, Octavia's father, and Agrippina, Nero's mother, the pair had grown up as half-sister and half-brother. Their union arranged by Agrippina had been useful to her purpose of establishing Nero's succession as Caesar.

All this I knew. Yet the old man looked at me with derision, as if I knew nothing.

"You seek Octavia?" he asked. "Not many do, you know, and still maintain the good regard of Caesar."

"It is but for a trifling thing," I replied.

I was becoming annoyed, and not a little anxious. I could not risk an argument here with this old man, or raise my voice to tell him what I thought of his rudeness.

He spat on the ground. "You follow that passageway to the end," he said at last. He nodded in the direction of the tunnel which I had already noted. "There you ask for Octavia."

"I am grateful," I said politely and bowed my head.

I left the old man as quickly as possible, knowing that he still watched me. If he expressed his curiosity to a guard, I would be followed. I walked into the passage half expecting to hear a heavy tread behind me.

Instead, I heard the echo of a shout from far down the passage. The place was deserted and dark, lit fitfully here and there by torches projecting from the wall. It was a long tunnel, with the far exit obscure.

Then I did hear the tread of feet, many of them. They came not from behind, but from the direction in which I was going. Again a shout came, this time repeated, echoing down the corridor. It seemed to be "Hail Caesar!"

My knees turned weak. I saw flickering torches ahead. Caesar approached! The passageway was scarcely wide enough for six or seven men to walk abreast.

My impulse was to turn and run. I could imagine no greater danger than to meet Caesar face to face in this narrow space. Would he demand my identity? Would he be angry at my unexplained presence, or even order my imprisonment or death for being where I should not be?

But if I ran back, my guilt would be established. And I could not hide in the solid walls of the passage.

I proceeded forward, assuming a pace as purposeful as I could command. A phalanx of soldiers approached, carrying torches held high. Their footsteps echoed down the hollow corridor, and they shouted at intervals for all to hear.

"Hail Caesar! All hail, Caesar!"

The first line of soldiers marched with swords drawn. As the long fingers of light from the torches reached out, I stopped walking and drew in tight against the wall. I stayed near a torch fixed above me to show that I was not attempting concealment, and I spread my arms to prove that I had no weapons.

In that moment of waiting, not knowing whether one of their blades would sever my neck and remove my living presence from the Emperor's annoyance, I might have wished that I was back in Colossae in the security of Philemon's villa. I did not. Even if I had to die at Caesar's feet, I thought, I could not regret my crimes.

I thought of Aurelia, and held my breath while the first soldiers marched past. A second line came up. The blades flashed bright under the torchlight. Each stern-faced Praetorian turned his head to look at me. They seemed to sear my face on their memories.

In the midst of the phalanx came Caesar, and I was surprised that Nero appeared almost as young as I. His hair was curly and yellow, his face shaven. He was heavy in figure, and his head rested on a thick, short neck.

I hoarsely uttered the words, "Hail, Caesar!" Startled, Nero turned his head, and for an instant his pale blue eyes met mine in the torchlight. His lips already hung apart, and I thought he was about to speak. But he did not, and walked on.

A number of friends followed him, most of them young men. Several laughed together loudly. They moved by in the glare of the torches, and suddenly I realized that the last rear guard of soldiers had passed.

Not one had stopped to ask my business here. I was still alive and whole.

I breathed deeply with relief. The cries of "Hail Caesar!" receded. Shakily, I resumed walking down the corridor.

The tunnel opened out to the sky after a time, and I was again in the fading evening light. A star brightened overhead. I found an entrance in the wall to my right, where an old man sitting on a stool was on guard.

"I seek the apartment of Octavia," I said.

"What do you wish there?" he asked.

I held up my letter. "I was sent on a matter of business."

He did not trouble himself to read the letter. He merely waved to me to pass on through the gate.

I found myself in a silent garden, deserted of people and filled only with palm trees and growing plants. The sounds of the city did not reach this far.

Then I heard music coming through the darkness. Did I imagine the notes of Aurelia's lyre? I noticed a torch burning above a door leading in from the garden, and with fast-beating heart I made my way toward it.

At the door, a woman stopped me. She was old and bent. I held out my letter, and she took it to read. When she had finished, she looked up at me. "You are sent by one whose name we have heard before," she said. "You have the jewels with you? Perhaps indeed my mistress would be amused by them."

She took the letter and disappeared. I heard her mounting steps; and meanwhile, that same soft music reached my ears from an upper floor.

The woman did not return for a long time. When she did finally come, she no longer held the letter.

"You may go up," she told me. "It is a good time now."

One can imagine with what feelings I followed her up the stairs. I doubt that I breathed in my anxiety. The woman led me into a room filled with soft light. There a young woman lay stretched on a couch in the center of the room, and two girls combed the long tresses of her hair.

This was Octavia. Indeed, no one had to tell me. She had a pale beauty and a wistful face. Her eyes seemed strikingly full of sadness. She held in her right hand my letter of introduction.

I crossed the floor toward her, without daring to turn my head. Suddenly the music I had been hearing faltered—stopped. Octavia glanced beyond me toward the corner of the room.

Then I looked also.

Aurelia!

She stood with another girl, each holding a lyre. The second one said, "Aurelia, I cannot keep accompaniment with you when you do not play."

But Aurelia stared at me. Her fingers were rigid across the strings of the lyre. And I—I know only that the whole room reeled and rocked as in a storm at sea and my eyes clouded so that I could see nothing but her face framed in an aura of tears in my eyes.

Octavia interrupted the spell. "Aurelia, are you ill?" she demanded. "Why do you not play?"

"Forgive me, mistress," Aurelia said quickly. "There was a cramp in my fingers. They are well now."

"Then play, please, and do not disappoint me."

Octavia looked back at me. Happily for the fortunes of both Aurelia and me, she had not noticed my expression or understood the recognition passing between us.

Only one had seen, as far as I could tell at that moment. One of the girls brushing Octavia's hair caught the significance of Aurelia's lapse in playing. I knew it by the troubled way in which this girl looked at both of us afterwards.

Only later did I wonder what had happened to the old woman who had led me upstairs. I had not been aware of her since I had entered through the door. Yet I had not heard her go away. Had she returned downstairs, or had the old guardian remained long enough to understand the shock in Aurelia's face and the joy in mine?

I recovered as quickly as Aurelia did. I dropped to one knee. "Hail, Octavia, wife of Caesar," I began.

She motioned for me to stand. "You are called Epaphras of Antioch?" she said. "It is you who is spoken of in this letter?"

"Yes, mistress," I replied.

The music continued softly, so that our conversation could be heard plainly above it.

I felt acutely Aurelia's presence. I hoped fervently that she caught the difference in my name.

"My father sent me to Rome to learn the ways of trade," I said boldly. "Then one day I may follow him in his business at Antioch."

There—that would tell Aurelia the lie I was living.

"You have jewels to sell?" Octavia asked.

"Yes, mistress, at your pleasure. These are stones which my father collected long years ago, perhaps even his father before him. I believe that they were acquired from time to time on journeys to Alexandria."

"Your father's love for his son must be great," she said. "He trusts you with his treasures."

"He has said, mistress, that a wise son is the greatest treasure of all. I am to use the proceeds from the jewels to buy clothing to improve my appearance, and books to improve my mind."

"Ah," Octavia cried, delighted. "You speak well, Epaphras of Antioch. I feel most willing to help you, even before I examine your jewels."

One of the serving girls brought a cushion, and I poured the gems from the bag across it. Exclamations of joy came from the girls and their mistress as the stones rolled out, catching the light from the lamps in the room. The two musicians, however, continued playing until Octavia lifted her hand to silence them, so that they too might see the jewels.

Aurelia came hesitantly. As the other serving girls leaned over the cushion beside Octavia's couch, I remained standing. I was able to hold Aurelia's glance with my eyes for a brief moment, and in that instant I tried to pour out all the longing I had kept for so long in my heart. Her face, her blue eyes, the long black strands of her hair were the same after the years. My joy put me into a delirium. I was more intoxicated than if I had drunk deeply of wine.

I received from her no answering expression. Once she had recovered from her first shock, she showed no further emotion.

The rebuff hurt. So long I had waited and searched for her. It was easy now to make myself believe that I had traveled all those miles from Colossae only to find her, that I had chosen a fugitive's life for her sake alone. Easily I forgot that Aurelia was still a slave, and more than a common slave. She belonged to the Emperor's wife. So thoughtlessly I put her into the dangerous position of shielding a runaway—and a runaway who was offering stolen jewels to the wife of Caesar. Aurelia would have deserved death merely for knowing me. Yet I blamed her for not acknowledging my smile.

Octavia looked up from the jewels on the cushion. She must have seen something strange in my face, and her glance went at once to Aurelia. But Aurelia did not give herself away.

"Do you not like these jewels, Aurelia?" Octavia asked. "You do not seem interested."

"Excuse me, mistress," Aurelia answered. "I have seen others like these in Asia. I have been at Ephesus where there is much trading in jewels."

"I had forgotten. Sometimes I do not remember how much life you had before you were given to me. You have seen so much more than I have myself. Tell me which of these stones I should buy."

"It is your choice, mistress."

"But I like all—this great ruby so glowingly red, the sapphire, the onyx carved into the odd shape. What is the meaning of the shape of this onyx, Epaphras?"

"I do not know, mistress," I replied. "Perhaps one may read into it a meaning of one's own."

"I will take it!"

I bowed, and smiled. The slave girls of Octavia selected first one stone and then another. They held them up to the light and watched with delighted exclamations as they glowed and glittered.

Each girl was dressed in a silken tunic with a girdle of gold, and wore a golden band around her hair. Each one had a quality of gentility, a manner equal to the highest rank. Their complexions were creamy white, their beauty complete perfection. I could see that, like Aurelia, they had been trained for their roles. They were meant to match the beauty and perfection of their mistress. Octavia had the kindest, most gentle nature, and I could understand why the people of Rome held her in such esteem and love.

The girl who guessed at the recognition between Aurelia and me was the most demure of all. She kept her eyes averted, and I knew that from her I had nothing to fear. I learned her name from words spoken to her by the others—Florentina. No dream could have foretold how great a part Florentina would play in the destinies of Aurelia and me.

The attention I paid to Octavia's selection of gems was scarcely a credit to my ability in selling. My mind was all on Aurelia, and I had to be called back twice to the business at hand. Octavia was most generous in the offer she made to me, I believe especially for the benefit of my welfare.

I replaced in the bag the jewels which remained. The

two girl musicians moved back to take up their lyres. The music began again, and Florentina and her companion resumed the dressing of Octavia's hair.

"Our thanks to you, Epaphras, for the joy of seeing such treasures," Octavia said. "We will remember you by what you have left for us. If you will go to the writer of this letter which introduced you, we will see to it that in two or three days your money will be in his hands. Meanwhile, Florentina will give you a token payment."

The slave girl went quickly to a chest at one side of the room. Octavia held out her hand from her reclining position on the couch, and I knelt to take it. I bent my head to kiss the delicate wrist. Surely, this first and lovely wife of Nero deserved a rightful share of imperial joys instead of the ghastly fate which was to fall upon her.

My audience was at an end. I rose to my feet, and Florentina placed coins in my hand. I had opportunity for only a brief glance in the direction of my loved one. She never turned her head to me.

I bowed again and backed out of the room. There was nothing more that I could do. I descended to the lower floor, where the old guardian woman was waiting for me. She took me to the door, and let me pass into the night.

The eyes of that old woman were inscrutably blank. If she had ill thoughts or intentions about me, I never knew. She may well have been the one to betray me later, on suspicion. I cannot tell. She was only one of those who might have done so.

Making my way across the garden, through the palm trees and shrubs, I heard again the music from the upper floor. This time voices of the girls blended with the notes of the lyres. There was Aurelia. At that moment I wished that I had never discovered her whereabouts.

Oh, bitter fortune that falls on human lives! That

night in the palace garden, unseen and unsuspect, I fell to the ground and clutched the earth in my hands as Aurelia's song drifted through the palms. I sobbed in the grass, and my tears ran in wild despair.

Later, I found my way back through the dark streets of the city. In the rotting dimness of a poor tavern, I lost my senses in wine. I spent the coins of Octavia, and neither knew nor cared what I said in that public place.

By morning I was again in my rented room. I do not know how I came to be there. Perhaps, without realizing it, I had brought misfortune upon myself by saying too much.

It did not seem to matter. My faith in everything was gone now, even in the love I had cherished through the years.

Later in that same day I was recognized by the one person in Rome whom I had fully forgotten. I was passing along the street with an ache in my head from the wine, and that feeling of old cloth in my mouth. A man approached me; and I was caught unawares. The man was Vergilio, the trader of Rome who had dealt with Philemon.

He came striding ahead, and he looked at me full in the face. It was too late for escape. Miraculously, I kept my composure without twitching even one muscle. He may have been thinking of other things, or perhaps remembrance of a slave out of past experience in another country meant nothing. He did not know me at all. He continued walking.

But a few steps behind Vergilio was Gulda, the girl slave.

She knew. At least she believed she did, for to her quick start of recognition I gave no response. My face was stony, and her exclamation checked itself halfway. I am certain she turned to stare after me, but I kept on walking.

What would she do? I dared not think. I was in a turmoil of foreboding.

It was as well. Nothing but my own fear saved me that night.

XII

I knew why they had come from the first moment I heard them. For a long time I had been standing in the cold night draft at the window of my room. I had beforehand a premonition that this was going to happen. When I heard the heavy steps of the soldiers at the door of the house, I was not surprised.

Sweat broke out over my body even in the cold air. I heard the landlady's protests loud over muffled commands. Then she screamed.

More than once I stood at this window wondering what I would do if this time ever came. My thoughts then were idle, never really believing it could be. But I had planned more or less a path of escape, first from my window to the roof of a smaller shed at the back of the house, from there to a rear court, and thence to a very narrow passage between two adjoining houses. What lay beyond that passage, I did not know. I had never gone down there to look.

Now in the dark of the night, this way offered my only hope. There was no hiding place inside the house. The soldiers would ransack everything. I had no time at all to lose. Their pounding feet were already on the stairs.

The jump from the window to the roof below was long, and dangerous in itself. Only a man driven by terror would have attempted it. I seized my mantle and dropped it down first, hoping its bulk would break the force of my fall. Then I climbed through the window, letting myself down against the outside wall, holding to the sill. Soldiers were clumping nearer. I pushed out from the wall, and let go my hold. I scraped my face and hands as I went, and fell in a heap on the roof. The mantle did help to provide a cushioning, but even so for a moment I was dazed. I hoped that the sound of my fall had not been heard.

From the roof to the ground was easier. I clutched my mantle around my shoulders and jumped again. Without pausing, I started across the courtyard to the opening between the houses, guessing the direction in the dark and hoping there was nothing to trip me.

It took me a few seconds of fumbling along the wall to find the passage. In that length of time I was aware of torchlights in my room. There was shouting now and the confusion of noises seemed very close.

I moved slowly down the passage, feeling my way with my hands in the absolute dark. As I have said, I did not know where this passage led, if indeed anywhere at all. I realized full well that the soldiers with torches momentarily would be searching here.

At first I found only a blank wall at the end of the passage and I groaned in my heart. But no—another passage led to the left. This one was covered over, and it took me into a second courtyard. I was frantic now, like a hunted animal. A light shone in the rear room of a house, the kitchen as I discovered by looking through a window. A man sat there on a stool, asleep with his head resting on the table in front of him.

I found the door into the room. It was not locked, and softly I opened it and entered. On silent feet I moved across, behind the sleeping man. I held my mantle spread out, ready to throw it over his head if he awakened.

I was successful, or full of luck. I went through the room without even scraping my sandals on the floor, and proceeded into the front of the house. No lights were there, and I felt my way. It was not too difficult to reach the front door.

This was locked with heavy chains which held the door by a tenacious system of hooks. I had to discover in the dark how to unfasten them. In doing so, unfortunately I allowed one of the chairs to rattle. My hands were shaking too much for me to be careful.

"Yes?" the man in the kitchen called sleepily. "I will come."

I redoubled my efforts. A section of the chain fell to the stone floor with a clatter.

"Pietrio!" The voice was a woman's from the floor above. "Pietrio, someone is at the door. Perhaps it is the master."

"Yes, mistress," the man replied, still from the kitchen. "I am coming when I have the light."

The last chain fell from its hook. I opened the door, and the glorious freshness of open air struck my face. I made my exit, pausing only long enough to close the door again. Pietrio would have much to puzzle him.

I found myself on a street, lighter now than inside the house because of the star glow. I lost no time in moving away, and I did so none too soon, for the man Pietrio opened the door with a light in hand. He peered up and down for his supposed master.

I could not yet be sure where I was, but I hastened in a direction which I thought would take me away from the neighborhood of my lodging house. The labyrinth of streets and alleys in this section of Rome was confusing enough in the daylight, and at night nearly impossible to make out. I could hear nothing at all. Most people by now were asleep. Few pedestrians stirred abroad after dark in this city, for fear of marauders who lay in wait to rob and murder the unwary.

My position now was only slightly less precarious than when the soldiers came for me. I had to admit that I was lost. If anyone discovered me wandering aimlessly about the streets, I would be hard pressed for an explanation. Any night watchman would take me for a thief. Yet I had to find some place of refuge before dawn. By morning the authorities in Rome would surely have issued a general alarm for my arrest.

In this state of doubt, I heard shouting and laughter. Against the house walls of a cross street I caught the approaching glimmer of reflections from many flares. Soldiers would not be making such merriment. Probably it was a party of revelers homeward bound in a group for protection.

With my mantle wrapped securely around me against the cold, I made my way cautiously toward the approaching sound. The little street I was now in seemed a mere alley, and I took a chance that the group would not turn into it. At the corner I waited, pressed close against the shadows of the house.

I was right in all respects. The group was a party of young men, singing and laughing with total disregard for the sleep of citizens in the vicinity. Some were too drunk to walk steadily and leaned on the shoulders of others. Some carried the flares I had seen, and an aura of light spread around them. They continued along the wide street down which they had come.

I fell in behind them, not too close but near enough for anyone to think that I was a straggler from the group. I pretended an unsteady walk too. I realized that I placed myself in a new danger, that of assault by bandits who could be following the revelers to capture just such stragglers as I appeared to be. My protection lay in keeping within the outer circle of torchlight.

The group, wherever they were going, helped me to locate myself. After several turns I discovered that we were crossing the square before the Pantheon. The great building was dark against the night sky.

I quickened my pace, and bore off to one side of the group, not daring to fall behind. Once more I managed to lose myself in the darkness. Hastily I found the comparative protection of housefronts.

From here I did indeed catch glimpses of shadowy forms following the revelers, like jackals in the night. Even as I noticed them, the revelers themselves overtook another party, a litter under escort of slaves.

What happened then, I could only guess. I heard sounds of confused scuffling, shouts, and a woman's scream of fear. A man groaned and there was the gurgle of death. The flares came together making a brighter glow, and a voice shouted merrily, "Let Caesar have her!"

In the brilliant flarelight I saw that the figures following the party were not marauders at all. They were soldiers of the Praetorian Guard in full regalia. Instead of assisting the party which had been attacked, they stood back, waiting at attention.

The revelers I had followed included the Emperor, out for a night of brawling. The soldiers were to protect him. I had heard rumors of such activities on Nero's part, always in whispers among the citizens of Rome.

I edged away from the dangerous vicinity of the Pantheon. At least, now, I knew my way. I made up my mind to get out of the city, somehow. Perhaps for a time I could take to the hills and hide there.

But as I stole through the black streets, I thought more into the future. What did Rome offer me now? I had no home. I had no employment, for I dared not go to Barea again. I was a hunted man who would have more difficulty than ever to establish himself. In the city my false papers were valueless, even incriminating, for my assumed name would be in the government records.

I did not know who had betrayed me or the extent of

the betrayal. Perhaps the soldiers had come to take me merely on suspicion for questioning, probably under torture. Perhaps some stranger had wondered about me, or even Barea, or Yrujo the Spaniard, who thus could keep for himself the money he had for me and which now I could never collect. Or possibly the old guardian woman of Octavia's quarters had caused the Praetorian Guard to follow me. Could I suspect Gulda? Who could know?

It was of little importance who had told. Rome left me no future except the existence of a mad dog, chased and stoned at every turn.

Even the illusion and the hope of seeing Aurelia had vanished now, as a dream fades on awakening.

I must leave Rome, and Italy. I could seek safety in some outpost of Empire, in the shadowy edge of Caesar's influence in Africa or Gaul or even Britain. My papers of identification would carry me there, and my remaining jewels would give me the means to pay my way.

I decided to follow the Tiber down to the seaport city of Ostia. From there I could take ship once more to safety.

Without further waste of time, I turned toward the bank of the river which cuts through Rome. I was stealthy and cautious, and avoided every chance of danger whether from groups of pedestrians, or night patrols, or lurking, shadowy marauders. The sound of a scurrying rat froze me, and a cat that rubbed against the calf of my leg sent me whirling to face an imagined assailant.

I did not get lost again. I found the Tiber and crept along the embankment quay downstream. The greatest danger lay in passing the city wall, patrolled by guards. After watching and listening, I slipped around each soldier, and with the dawn I was in the open swamps of the Campagna, well west of the city.

I had counted on the dangers from man, but not those of nature. Walking through the tall dead grasses near the river, I found soft places of watery mud where I could easily have sunk forever from sight. Several times I had difficulty in pulling my sandaled feet from the sucking mire. The water was cold, and a chill wind blew across the flats from the sea. I felt my limbs growing numb.

The rising sun brought slight warmth and some relief, but the heat awakened the insects of the swamp. In brief time I was attacked by swarms of humming mosquitoes, and I had to use what was left of my strength to brush them away from my face. Exhaustion crept over me. I wished to rest, but the cold mud offered no place to lie down. I could not stand still because of the insects on my face and hands.

The Ostian Way to the south offered the comfort of solid ground but also the presence of traffic, and soldiers, and the certainty of arrest. A ship moved up the Tiber under sail, but its destination was Rome. A galley manned by sailors skimmed past, and I kept my head low among the grasses until they had gone from sight.

I kept walking, with each step slower and more painful than the one before. My eyes were closing from the swelling of insect stings. Lassitude crept over me. It seemed that it would be easy to lie down and be swallowed painlessly by the mud and cold water. Better than the tortures of the Romans. . . .

A fishing boat came along the river, with a small square sail and one man in the stern steering by an oar. I did not see him until it was too late.

"Stranger!" he called. "May God be with you, but what are you doing there?"

I staggered toward the river bank. The fisherman turned his craft swiftly toward shore, and I remember seeing him leap from his seat in the stern.

Then I fell forward in the mud.

I remember nothing more until I was in the boat, lying flat on the floorboards of the little vessel. The fisherman was washing my face with a cloth soaked in water of the Tiber.

I looked up into his face. He was rough and bearded, and he smelled of fish. Yet I had never been so grateful to anyone.

"You nearly finished yourself, my friend," he said when my eyes opened. "I have a swallow of wine for you. It will warm you. I believe you are as cold as a man can get and still keep his soul within him."

The wine burned down my throat. I was shivering with a chill like the ague, but gradually it went away. I had said not a word, for I had lost my voice. It occurred to me that I had not used it since before the soldiers came to my lodging, a long, long time ago it seemed. My throat felt paralyzed.

Lifting his oar, the fisherman pushed his boat from the bank into the stream. The wind whipped at the sail. Taking his seat in the stern, he said, "Going downstream? I suppose you are anxious to leave Rome?"

I nodded.

"A little trouble during the night? Makes the swamp look good compared to the city. I have seen it happen before. Next time, take to the hills, and not to the swamps of the Campagna. Lots go in there and stay there for all time!"

My rescuer pulled on the sail until the breeze tightened it. The craft began moving downstream again, almost sideways against the west wind.

"Whatever your trouble, it does not interest me," the fisherman said. "As long as you do not cause me any trouble here. *That* I would not try."

He seemed to expect an answer. I shook my head, emphatically.

"For the rest," he said, gazing down the channel of

the river, "you make your own peace with Christ in heaven."

I sat up straight. This man a Christian! He motioned to me to lower my head under the sail as he swung the bow of the boat into the breeze to come about.

"It is a long beat downstream against the west wind," he said. "Here comes a ship up from Ostia. It carries grain from Alexandria for Rome."

I turned to look. With sails set full, the ship sped down the center of the channel, white foam breaking at the bow.

"Make out that you are doing something," the fisherman said. "Work on the lines there. No use arousing curiosity about a fisherman like me carrying an idle passenger."

I did as I was told, pretending to untangle a coil of fishing line. The fisherman kept his craft from the ship's way, but so closely that I might have reached out to touch the larger vessel. Crewmen looked over the railing at us. We rocked in the wake.

"I will set you ashore downstream a distance," my rescuer told me. "There is a section of hard ground, and an old cabin if you want to sleep. It is tight enough to keep most insects away."

I looked at him gratefully. It seemed so strange that I could not find my voice to express thanks.

The fisherman watched the channel with keen and restless gaze. He drove the boat almost against the shore, then he pushed hard on his oar and swung the bow about. Back and forth we moved down the Tiber, with the current helping against the adverse wind.

I watched the man as he sat erect in the stern, his eyes sharp as an eagle's. The breeze blew at his beard, and his strong hands held the oar firm in the water. He had wild, rough characteristics, and yet a gentleness of manner which, strangely, made me think of Paul the apostle.

I cleared my throat. I had to speak. To be dumb of voice terrified me—I would be unable to ask for passage on a ship, or to make my way anywhere.

He noticed my efforts. "More wine," he said, and handed me the goatskin container.

I let the liquid settle into my throat. I only choked and had to spit the wine over the side of the boat.

"Do not be concerned," the fisherman said. "You suffer from shock. After you sleep, you will be recovered."

This man had a way of authority. I gave up trying to speak. The effort only paralyzed me the more.

"I can give you a word that will help you," he went on. "You suffer from a fear of the sin that you have done. I, too, once suffered in the same way. I was haunted night and day. I could not escape from myself, not on shore nor on the sea. I thought no one could equal the torment of sin which was mine."

He paused.

"After a time," he continued, "I found that there had been another who suffered more. That one had taken upon himself my sins, and all the other sins which any man had ever committed. His suffering was beyond description. That one died, leaving a message for me—for me, you understand? The message said that he died that I might live, if only I would believe it was so. Because he took my sin, I no longer had need to carry the guilt. I was forgiven, by believing."

I tried again to speak. I knew the one to whom he referred was Jesus Christ.

"Try to find that man," the fisherman said. "There are those will tell you of him. Seek for him yourself, rather than listen to me. You will find peace as I have."

I moved my lips.

"Should I tell you my sin?" he asked. "It was a great crime against my brother."

Another ship came flying up the river, and I went

back to fumble at the lines again. Once more we were rocked in the wake and sprayed with the running foam.

When the ship had passed, the fisherman stood up. He watched a bar in the river, and noted how the current swept in under a bluff on hard, dry land.

Without looking at me, he said, "You wish to know my crime? Perhaps it will be good for you, and for me also, if I tell it. I killed my brother."

He had driven the boat tight in under the bluff. The bow pushed itself against the bank, and the fisherman held it there with his oar against the pressures of wind and river.

"This is the place," he said. "Quickly—and God be with you and preserve you."

I saw a small building on the bluff set back from the river, a shack that was long deserted and falling down. I stood up in the boat and leapt ashore. With difficulty I climbed the slippery bank and looked back down from the top. The fishing boat was out in the stream again. The fisherman still stood in the stern, facing down river, firmly holding his oar.

"And the peace of God be with you!" I cried aloud. But the wind carried the words away, and the fisherman did not know that I had recovered my voice.

All through the day I slept in the shack, with the sleep of the exhausted near to death. I woke toward evening, and washed my face in the Tiber.

The wind had fallen, and the mosquitoes were out again. The weather had turned warmer. The sky was overcast, and an uneasy feeling of storm filled the air. I pulled my mantle around me, making sure that my documents and jewels were safe.

I walked across the distance lying between the river and the Ostian Way, the great highway between Rome and the seaport city. Darkness came early, and I felt reasonably safe. My weakness now was not from exhaustion but from hunger. I had eaten nothing for a full day and night.

The highway here was deserted; there were few houses and no traffic at this time of night. I walked in the direction of the coast for some time, and the only relief for my hunger was a roadside vineyard with a few post-season grapes still on the vines. To find these in the dark was a labor which starvation alone could justify.

My journey in the fishing boat had carried me a long way toward Ostia, so that by midnight I had reached the street of tombs outside the city. I thought it not advisable to enter by the first and nearest gate, called the Roman Portal. Therefore, I waited for the first light of dawn under a cloudy sky. Then I circled the city wall so as to enter at the marine gate beside the harbor.

This part of the town was crowded with sailors and stevedores, and no one thought to notice me. I passed the docks, and took account of the great number of ships tied up there, as well as of the several hundred more anchored out in the harbor toward the sea.

At a waterfront tavern I made a meal of dried fish, bread, and fresh oranges. I ate slowly, and to my fill. Pretending a language difficulty, I refused to be drawn into conversation with the seamen there.

After dining comfortably, I ventured briefly into the heart of the city to seek out a buyer for more of my jewels. Ostia, now some four hundred years old, is supposed by legend to have been founded on the landing place of Aeneas. Historically it has shared in naval wars, and now, situated strategically at the mouth of the Tiber, it is a part of Rome's defensive system. As the nearest seaport, Ostia maintains a heavy export and import trade, and through its harbor comes most of Rome's food supply.

I was much impressed with the size and number of grain warehouses, enough to provide for the entire city of Rome. I saw large houses containing apartments for many families, the palaces and villas of the wealthy, and a theater. By chance, I came across a temple of Mithra.

Possessed by some half-resentful curiosity, I entered the temple. It was a building long and narrow, and the customary holy sanctuary was underground in a basement. The place was entirely deserted and I was alone, but the holy fire glowed in a bed of embers on the altar.

I stood here for some minutes, endeavoring to find again the inspiration which Mithra had aroused in my youth. It was gone. The crypt seemed as hollow as the sound of my footsteps. The sacred carvings along the walls were no more than ornamental decorations, mocking the fallacious notions of mankind.

I could not say a prayer to Mithra. The God of Light had turned to ashes as cold as those which had fallen from the altar to the floor.

Before my eyes kept reappearing the wind-burned face of the Tiber fisherman as he spoke simply of Christ: *He died for me, that I might live.*

I hurried from the crypt. On the ground floor above, I met the red-robed priest of Mithra entering the building. I lowered my eyes and walked by, on into the street.

With a shudder I remembered the priest at Colossae who permitted the slaughter of the virgin on the altar— that she might atone for *her* sin.

He died that I might live, and be forgiven. . . . For the first time, I perceived as through an opening in the clouds one meaning of Christ's life on earth.

I had tested myself with Mithra. Instead of responding, I took a first step toward Christianity.

Sobered in mind, I returned to the waterfront. I should no longer risk delay in Ostia.

XIII

Near the quays I found a small shop that dealt in oddities of all kinds, and I was able to sell to the proprietors a handful of onyx stones. They asked me no questions. The price they gave me was far lower than it ought to have been, but I was not in a position to bargain.

Taking the money, I left the shop and walked along the waterfront. Ships lined the wharves, and so busy was the port that others waited at anchor for their turns to come in. Stevedores unloaded vessels and, while wagons and carts hauled goods away to the peril of pedestrians, other ships were being loaded. The constant activity of a rushing port resulted in the worst kind of confusion to one not familiar with marine affairs.

At last I saw a ship obviously nearly ready to sail. The crew were aboard, and freeing the yards. I spoke to a dockman and discovered that the vessel was destined for Gades in Spain.

Spain—the word brought visions. From travelers coming to Colossae, I had heard of Spain and its great size—greater than all of Italy. I knew that Gades was a large city on the far western, ocean side of Spain, an important port on the sea routes to Gaul and Britain. From Gades, I thought, I could go into the interior of the vast Spanish country, and there find for myself a new life.

I proceeded without delay to board the ship, crossing to the deck over the plank from the wharf. It was a large vessel, of some six or seven hundred tons burden.

Its mast stretched high, and the unfurled topsail already hung loosely in the slight breeze from the harbor.

I found the captain on the far side of the deck, giving final orders before casting off. I waited until I could interrupt him.

"You are sailing for Gades," I said. "That is my destination also, and I wish to take passage with you."

He looked at me briefly and nodded. "Yes, we have space for one more. You have money for passage?"

I settled with him on the spot, and he continued, "Now get your things aboard quickly. We leave immediately, to clear the wharf for another ship."

I did not tell him that I had no baggage. I walked up into the bow, and from there watched the crew working with the lines. There were a number of other passengers, I noticed, including a few women. I was relieved that no soldiers were aboard.

Inevitably my anxiety remained until the lines were cast free and the space of water between the ship and the dock began to widen. This was farewell to Italy—a far more abrupt departure than I had anticipated. I could not help the sharp pain in my heart as I thought of Aurelia. Beyond recall, I was putting her behind me forever. Yet I realized how impossible any other prospect had been from the start. I had been a fool in my optimism. Aurelia herself had made that much all too clear to me. Freedom for a slave—in security, comfort, or in love—had no more meaning than any other of the false ideals and illusions to which at one time or another I had been faithful.

Our ship dropped away from the waterfront of Ostia and pointed its bow toward the open sea beyond the protecting breakwater. The captain continued to shout orders, and I was surprised to notice that the square mainsail was not released. We moved across the harbor under only the small topsail, and little more than drifted in the calm air.

Suddenly the forward anchor rumbled out on its chain, and we came to rest.

With some alarm I asked a crewman about it.

"A storm is in the air," I was told. "The captain will wait in the harbor overnight."

I had enough experience to recognize the ominous quality of the atmosphere. The horizon was dark across the Tyrrhenian Sea, and the clouds overhead showed peculiar lines in their grayness. I would rather have seen the shore of Italy drop from sight as soon as possible, but I had no recourse but to curb my own impatience.

At this time of year, the season for navigation was nearing its end. Few captains ever ventured out on the sea during winter, and the usual practice was to seek shelter in a safe harbor until spring. But the autumn storm of which the warning was in the air turned out to be exceptionally disastrous for any season.

Our ship rode at anchor throughout that afternoon and on into the night. The captain and most of the crew took to sleeping, and the passengers did the same. I found a sheltered place on the deck and lay there with my mantle folded across me. The air was warm, humidly warm for that time of the year, and I rested.

All around us were other ships, some ready to depart as we were, but waiting for the weather. Others had arrived recently, and held themselves at anchor until a wharf became free. Still other ships turned into the mouth of the Tiber and disappeared on their journey to Rome.

The city of Ostia from this distance seemed detached and silent, like some sand creation of a child. The Alban Hills to the south of Rome and the more distant Sabines to the northwest were shielded by a luminescent haze of curious gray-blue color. The tall lighthouse on the mole at the harbor entrance stood forth black. The ship swung at anchor, and at last I fell asleep.

When I awakened, darkness had come. The ship

under me trembled from the short, violent blows of waves against the planking of the hull. I was cold from a fresh wind soaked with sea mist.

I started up. Something was wrong; something was happening. My feeling was borne out when I saw the captain signaling to crewmen far up the mast securing the sails. Under flickering torchlight, other sailors ran across the decks. Everything loose was being fastened down or removed.

I saw lights from the city of Ostia, and other lights from ships across the harbor. The lamp in the lighthouse on the mole outshone the rest. But overhead was the dense blackness of a threatening night. From far over the sea came a rumbling noise like subdued thunder.

Other passengers on the vessel had disappeared, gone below deck, I supposed. I sought shelter by the lee side cabin on the forecastle, and stayed there with my mantle wrapped close. The wind increased and I could make out white foam cresting the waves below. A sheet of rain blew over, then stopped. The noise like thunder increased. Looking down the length of the ship, I perceived through the wavering shadows the figure of the captain running. A sailor held a torch high on the foredeck, and the wind caught the flame and pulled it out in long streamers of sparks over the ocean.

A group of sailors struggled forward carrying a heavy burden. Another held a torch for them, and I saw that the men were bringing up from astern a second anchor. They crossed the foredeck.

The storm hit all at once and with fearful impact. The vessel shuddered throughout. Slowly, under heavy pressure of the mighty wind, the boat rolled until it lay far on its side. Two of the sailors slipped and I saw their arms reach out helplessly as they went overboard. A torrent of rain descended, and it became almost impossible to see down the deck.

I heard cries from below. I reached out for myself to find something to which I could cling for safety, and discovered what seemed to be a life raft. It rested on edge, and it was secured by hooks and chains to the side of the cabin. There were loose ends of ropes attached to the raft, and I grasped them quickly. Although my hands turned numb in the cold rain, yet I managed to tie myself to that raft with a loose knot which I could release instantly if I had need. For caution's sake, I found out with my hands in the dark how to disengage the raft with all speed if necessary.

The wind rose upon us, and I heard through the darkness the sharp sounds of ship's equipment giving way. The boat swung on its anchor with its prow into the gale, so that it righted itself. Now the force of the storm swept down the length of the deck. I braced myself against the sting of the rain, the violence of the tempest.

A ship to the lee of us suddenly showed a burning bright glow in its heart. Red fire flashed through openings, and heat turned the deluge of rain to steam. Sparks burst up—then flames. Driven by the relentless wind the fire spread through the ship in a matter of moments, roared into the open air above the deck, and rose high to lick with consuming tongue the rigging of the mast. Each sail burst into flame and vanished. A heavy cloud of sparks whipped away on the wind, and it was possible to see dark shapes jumping into the sea from the decks, some of them themselves flaming torches.

That vessel fell apart in a glowing inferno and turned over. The sea poured in, and a violent explosion of steam and sparks subsided slowly into darkness again.

In the distance another vessel caught fire. As a huge torch, its light flickered against the low-flying clouds close overhead. The flames were reflected across the wild sea, and the endless foam turned red as blood.

Most terrifying of all, a massive silent shape drove close by our bow. I could have thrown a stone into it from where I stood. It was a helpless vessel demasted and stripped of rudder, and driven before the gale. It vanished in the dark.

The storm came out of the west, in from the open sea, and the harbor's breakwaters offered no protection at all. Many ships crashed against the rocks that night, and others foundered at the docks of Ostia. It was a titanic disaster, and few living men could remember a storm so terrible. Indeed it seemed that the prophecies of the Jews were being fulfilled, and the end of the world had come.

Through the holocaust I remained remarkably calm. I knew that we were in fearful danger. It seemed that no vessel on the face of the waters could withstand the fierceness of that storm. Yet among the anguished cries from below and the death and destruction apparent all over the harbor, at first I had no feeling at all. I had done what could be done for my safety. There was no more fleeing for my own account. If I died, as I was likely to die, I would die this night no more alone than the many others who were dying, too.

I wondered about death as it came near. Everyone, I thought, must die alone, despite the company with him. It is each man's private affair, a matter that had to be met by oneself. It makes little difference how one dies, on one's own couch, or under the sword, or in the waters of the sea. The pain may be greater or lesser, but the act of dying is the same. It has to be a lonely act.

Yet under the canopy of death that night, it came to me that I was wrong. No man of that great fleet would die as lonely as I. I had no more of an identity than some block of wood washed ashore. Here I was not Onesimus, or even Epaphras, or anyone at all. If I died under these waves, no one could guess what body it was. Those who had known me during my years would never hear that Onesimus of Colossae, or the slave boy purchased in Antioch, or Epaphras, son of Julius Dorius, had perished in the storm. No one could ever know.

The captain of the ship, if he died, would be with his ship. The women below would be in company with their men; and the men with their women. There were the others with families ashore, relatives who would share the loss and would mourn.

If every man has to die alone, at least he can die with meaning in the world he left behind. It was a queer thought for me in facing death that I had disassociated from myself any earthly meaning at all.

Or heavenly meaning, either. I had repudiated all gods and all ideas of existence for my soul in any eternal place. Yes, I thought, of all the company with which I would die that night on the sea, I would die the most alone.

Only then did I feel terror. It is a fearful thing to have to die as much alone as I was then. I cried aloud in terror. The cry blew away unheard. The sweat on my brow washed away in the rain. I strained at the knot holding me, and would have plunged straightaway into the sea.

The ship suddenly shook, and the deck gave away. The hull rose partly out of the water, and a tremendous sound of crackling and splintering burst over everything, increasing to a terrible roar that completely filled my numbed ears, smothering even the screaming below and on deck.

I saw that the entire stern of the vessel was being sheared away by another drifting ship. In the force of the collision both crafts were breaking rapidly apart. This was it—this was dying.

I stood transfixed. Amidships shadowy forms appeared and leaped over the rail. Someone appeared with a flaming torch. People ran aimlessly. Several rushed up to the forecastle and came around to where I was.

I reached out to seize one man.

"Hold here!" I shouted at the top of my voice. "The safest place . . . !"

A woman was with the man, clinging to his waist. I gave them each an end of rope fastened to the raft. At that moment our mast fell, and in falling it crashed astern into the already splintered wreckage of both boats. Our ship was rolling over.

I remembered in time to cast loose the chains holding the raft to the cabin wall, and we fell forward across the sloping deck. I know that I was struck by something, and my next sensation was of being plunged deep into cold water.

I did not attempt to struggle. This was death, and of what avail was it to struggle against death?

But in that moment—strangely—I believed that I heard the voice of Paul the apostle. Clearly in my ears filled now with rushing water I heard him say, *"God preserve you and bless you, in the grace of the Holy Spirit."*

It was a trick of the mind, of course. It is said that the mind of a drowning man does strange things. But the steadfast face of Paul flashed before me, and his penetrating voice rang as clearly as if I were again in the little room of his house.

I breathed fresh air. I gasped and choked up salt water. A great wave washed over me, and once more I gagged for breath. It passed, and I felt myself being tossed high on a crest of foam.

The two persons who had been with me were gone. I believe I saved myself in that first deep plunge into the sea by not struggling against the knot that tied me to the raft.

I remember very little more. I lost sense of direction and of time. I existed on that piece of board, learning to breathe between the waves that rolled over my inert body. My fingers were too numb and my arms too weak to do anything else. I had no sense of other ships, or of people swimming in the water, and I had no spirit to call for help. I could see nothing because of the water in my smarting eyes, except that once I was blinded by a great light above me. In half consciousness, I decided that it must be the lighthouse, and I was being carried out to sea by a perverse current even against the wind.

Slowly the cold crept more deeply into my body, and I lost all feeling in my limbs. I would die slowly then. The numbness coming from my legs into my body was death.

I did not mind so much. The vision of Paul remained in my mind. Now I was not so lonely in meeting this forgetfulness called death. I remembered that Paul had once said, *We pray always for the state of all men, in the name of Jesus Christ the Lord.*

As I passed into death, I could believe that I was not entirely forgotten, after all. Christ had died, too.

My first spark of consciousness picked up the sound of voices, coming and going away in my ears. The voices annoyed me, and I kept wishing that they would stop so that I might return to sleep.

Then I felt that I was being lifted by the legs. This annoyed me also, but I had not enough strength to resist. I moved my head in protest, and had it shoved firmly to one side by someone. I vomited water, and I felt the salt in my nose.

I think I slept again, but after a time those persistent voices awakened me further. I opened my eyes, and the light was too bright. My legs were being held, and my feet raised and lowered, rather like the slow motions of a pump handle. I grunted, and threw up more water which rolled warmly over my neck.

Another voice joined the first ones. I recognized it to be a woman's. She had not fallen off the raft, after all? I was very confused. I was being rolled up in something warm, my legs and my body. I put out my arms to steady myself and felt damp sand under my hands.

I opened my eyes again.

My blurred vision made out two men leaning over me. One held my legs, while the other wrapped me in a blanket. The woman was somewhere behind them.

"Bring him to the house," she was saying.

"Not yet," said the man holding my legs. "He has to lose more water."

With that I vomited again. It was as if the sea were rolling back out of my chest. I coughed violently, and brought up more. I saw now that I was lying on a sandy beach.

I had not drowned. I was still living.

I was too weak to keep my eyes open for long. And I had to clear my mind. I remembered only the wash of water over my head in the dark night as I drifted alone on the raft. Alone? Yes, for the woman here could not be the same as the one who had been on the ship. She and the man must have drowned.

Many, many persons must have drowned. I shuddered. I felt myself going to sleep again.

"He is too cold. You should bring him in," the woman said. "We will make him warm."

"Yes, it is time."

The two men lifted me from the beach, without ceremony or pardon.

"Where am I?" I tried to cry out. I succeeded only in a choked mutter.

"On the beach," answered the man who held my legs.

"You were dead," the other man said, marveling. "You were dead, and we have brought you to life. It is a miracle."

"No miracle but work," the first one scoffed.

"It is a miracle that he was carried by the tide all this

distance to us," the woman said. "Between here and Ostia is nothing but swamp where no one lives."

For the first time I was able to see her. She was plainly dressed in a gray wool tunic. Her hair was coiled at the back of her head, and her hands showed the harshness of work.

They lived in a small stone building up from the beach. As they carried me, I noticed nets and lines drying on racks in front of the house. There were also many stacks of cut and split wood.

I could not dispute their carrying me into their house. My strength was utterly gone.

I was borne into the one big room, and placed on a bedding of straw against the wall. A fire roared on the hearth, and the air was hot and close. It felt good to me. Another woman was there in the house, and as soon as they brought me in she took a caldron of hot water from the fire. She was young, with soft yellow hair and blue eyes. Her smile of sympathy was full of sweetness.

The two women proceeded at once to disrobe me, and in my naked state they washed me with warm water mixed with oil. I felt the life returning to my body under their massaging hands. I lost more sea water and slowly began to breathe normally.

When they had finished, they wrapped me in the blanket again and turned my face to the wall. There I slept—for how long I cannot say.

When I awakened, the four of them were gathered around a large bowl of soup, and darkness was outside. A candle burned on the table, and the far corners of the room were lit with the warm light of the flickering fire. They invited me to share their food. Clad in my blanket, I sat with them and ate of the soup and bread. I was nearly starved, as I had had nothing to eat since that morning in Ostia—was it only a day before?

In a state of high tension, I tried to talk about the storm and the sinking ships. Already they had heard the story of the disaster at Ostia—two hundred ships in all were destroyed, they said. It was the worst tempest that had ever been known in this area, they told me. Yet they would not let me speak of the ship on which I sailed, or of the collision, or of the fires aboard the others. They would hear it another time, they said. I must not remember now.

They were kind to me, those people. I found that they were two brothers living here with their wives. They cut wood for their living, and they fished to add to their sustenance.

I asked them for my mantle, and learned that it was gone. The men who had found me unconscious and still tied to the raft had seen nothing of any clothing washed up on the beach. I myself had been as if dead, half naked, with my tunic ripped. Even my sandals were gone, torn off by the waves.

My girdle with its sack of jewels, my documents, my money—all were lost. I had nothing.

To have been drowned and lost forever in the infinite spaces of the Tyrrhenian Sea would have been preferable to being adrift in the living world with no identity at all.

XIV

The woodchoppers shared their clothing with me and furnished me with sandals. I shaved my beard, too, and became presentable again. The women gave generously of their food, although these were poor people and had little to spare.

On the third day that I was with them, my strength

was far recovered. In the morning I ventured out to work with the brothers, hoping to repay them with my labor. Undoubtedly the experience with the sea had done much to chasten my character. I was no longer the hopelessly selfish ingrate of other days.

A quantity of timber was being washed ashore each day from the catastrophe at Ostia. The woodcutters hastened to the beach to make the most of what could be salvaged. I worked to help them collect usable pieces and pile them in stacks above the mark of the high tide.

Also I looked without success for any trace of my own belongings. The sea had irretrievably claimed them.

The wife of one brother, the older woman, came also to work on the beach.

"There is little which you should do," she told me in all kindness. "You do not have the strength that you think."

"Indeed, I do have," I said boldly. "To help your husband and his brother is the least that I can do for you."

Yet even in full health I would have had no strength to compare with that of the brothers. Under the warm sun they worked stripped except for the cloths girded around their loins. Their great muscles rose in knots on their shoulders and flowed like whipcord across their backs. As they worked, they chanted an ancient woodchoppers' song.

The two together lifted and carried the heaviest timbers and long planks which the waves had cast ashore. I had to content myself with smaller splinters and broken pieces.

I found a great satisfaction in work on that beach. The sand was clean and the sun warming. I had the companionship of contented people. These woodchoppers had a peace in their own hearts which I had seldom known in other people. I wondered whether it was because they knew nothing else than their own simple existence, or whether they had indeed found a security in life too deep for easy perception.

It occurred to me that I might be glad to live a life like theirs. How far the lot of the woodchopper would be from my earlier dreams of fine possessions and great fortune! But the question of what I must in fact do next was serious. My survival from the shipwreck, ironically, had left me helpless. I had no further place to go. Without money or papers, I could plan nothing. I was at the end of the road. Perhaps the best thing for me to do would be to settle here, and at least be thankful that I remained alive.

To be alive at all was indeed a miracle, as I realized more and more. When I looked across the stretch of the Tyrrhenian Sea toward the distant light tower of Ostia and saw how far I had drifted, the sense of a miracle grew stronger.

But a miracle must be wrought by some power, as compared with mere chance which brings happenings without cause or purpose. If my existence was due to a miracle, then what power had wrought it? I remembered that the Christian Paul had been said to perform miracles. And I had thought of Paul and felt the strength of his presence as I went down into the sea.

Had Paul inadvertently wrought the miracle which saved my life?

While I carried wood in my arms across the soft sand, I remembered more: Epaphras saying that miracles were wrought not by men but by God in heaven through the agency of men on earth whom God had especially chosen.

Such thoughts of unknown things sent terror into my heart. I dropped my armload of wood onto the stack, and paused a moment to gaze over the sea.

"You are thoughtful, friend," one of the brothers said on their next trip to the stack.

"It is nothing," I said. "I was thinking about miracles."

"Miracles? Only the gods perform miracles. What indeed is a miracle, after all?"

"I know of miracles," his brother said. "The sun crossing the sky each day, the fish breathing under water, the fact of life from out of a woman—are not these things miracles of the gods?"

"Our visitor was thinking of the miracle of his life preserved," the woman guessed. She had just come up from the water line, and she dropped an armful of knots on the woodpile.

"No miracle that," the first brother scoffed. "He happened to drift here, and we found him in time to pull him back from death. No miracle. Not unless you are of such value that the gods must preserve you by a miracle of their doing."

"No," I replied. "No, I am not of such value."

"He is different from us," the woman said. "He comes from a world beyond our knowing. We must not trouble him."

"He is different, yes," the second brother agreed. "A woodcutter never stops his work to look at the sea."

The man did not intend his remark to be unkind. He merely stated a fact.

"It is time that he stopped working," the woman said. She looked at me. "You have done enough for today. You may work with us again tomorrow. Now the wife of my husband's brother has prepared hot broth at the house."

"No," I said, "I will keep on working. I will look no more at the sea." Then I added to all of them, "You speak of tomorrow. Already I have troubled you for three days."

"Your strength was far gone," the woman said. "You need time yet."

"You are welcome here," one of the brothers said simply.

They returned to their work.

As I went down to the edge of the shore for more wood, I thought hard on settling in this place. I had not seen other houses near, or people who might become curious about me or report to the authorities the presence of a suspicious person. As far as I knew, the wood-cutter family lived alone in this place between the sea and the forest. Perhaps I could build a hut for myself further down the beach. The materials for a habitation were spread for the asking along the shore. The brothers would help if I asked.

The idea of remaining grew in my mind. But all at once I saw other people further down the beach, like us searching for salvage. There were perhaps a score of them, slowly moving in our direction.

"Who are they?" I asked the woman.

"Our neighbors," she said. "They live further back in the forest, a small settlement of them. Some are fishermen, others woodcutters like ourselves."

The first of the group approached, with their heads bent low as they searched for useful things washed ashore.

"I believe I am tired, after all," I said to the woman. "I will go back to the house. Tomorrow I can be more useful."

She nodded. "I thought so. It is too soon for you to do hard work."

I left the beach before any of the strangers saw me. My hosts and rescuers had not yet asked me one word about who I was, or where I had been going, or from whence I had come before the storm. They accepted me without question. They did not show the usual human curiosity, but instead cared for their affairs and let me care for mine.

Neighbors might not be as courteous. Inevitably, they would wonder about a new settler in their midst. They would ask questions. Rumors would begin.

At the house I found the young wife sweeping the floor.

"I thought that you would come," she said. "I have prepared broth for your strength. It is made from good fish."

She laid down the broom and went to bring me a bowl of the soup. I sat on a stool, and she stood watching while I drank it. New strength worked through my body as I swallowed the warm liquid.

"You are pretty," I said. "I like the yellowness of your hair."

"Thank you," she said with a smile.

"I have not met many women with such hair and blue eyes."

"We are from the north," she explained. "Have you been in the north?"

I shook my head. "I have been to the east," I said cautiously. "The women I know have dark hair, thick and heavy. Their eyes may be dark—or they may be deep blue like a pool at twilight." I was thinking of Aurelia.

"I have not seen a woman with dark hair and blue eyes," she answered.

"I know only one."

I finished the soup.

"You too are different from the men of the north," she said. "You have seen much of the world, have you not?"

"Some. In what way am I different?"

She lowered her gaze. "I do not know myself, but I have not met any one like you."

"Do you think I could become a woodcutter?"

"No, you are not meant for a woodcutter," she said. "Or even a fisherman. You are not—not strong." She laughed as she added, "Like my husband. You should work with your mind, not your hands."

"I could become strong."

"No. It is too late. One is born to be a woodcutter, as I was born to be the wife of a woodcutter."

She walked to the corner of the room. I followed.

She stopped before a niche built into the wall. Two small carved figures were there, representations of youths dressed in short tunics pulled above the knees. Each figure held a drinking cup in one hand and a wine beaker in the other. The carvings I recognized to be Lares, gods of the household.

"Whose are these?" I asked.

"This one belongs to my husband and to me," she said, pointing to the figure on the left. "We shall take it when one day we have a house of our own. The other Lar belongs to my husband's brother and his wife."

"Do you believe in them?"

"Of course. Each morning my husband and I pray together for our fortune and the early establishment of our own home. This is what every woodcutter does."

"There are no such gods as your Lares," I said rashly. "They are figures meaning nothing at all."

"You dare not speak thus in a woodcutter's home," she cried.

I did not mean to offend her by what I said next, but I was suddenly driven on by great urgency. I did not anticipate what would happen.

"Have you heard of the God Jehovah?" I asked.

"No."

"He is the only God. There are no others."

She moved away.

"You do not fear to say this God Jehovah is greater than Vesta, and Apollo and Mercury, as well as our Lar to whom we have always prayed?"

"That is not what I said. He is not greater or better than they are. They do not exist at all."

I was stubborn in my convictions.

"No Vesta, no Apollo, or Mercury?"

I was appalled myself at my own words. I stared at her and she at me.

"Are you serious in what you say?" she asked at last.

"Yes."

"I think you are serious." She hesitated. "When first you were brought here, I saw that you were not like us. You have seen what we have not, and you have knowledge that we have not. And during your long sleep, I heard you talk. I have told no one, but I knew that sin was heavy in your heart. I was glad that the gods had carried you here." She made a despairing gesture. "But now you speak things I cannot believe. By what sign do you say them?"

"The Lord God Jehovah sent his Son to live on earth as living testimony to the truth. His name was Jesus Christ."

"Why do you tell me these things? I owe my worship to Vesta, the protector of our hearth, and to our Lar who will provide a home for us."

"Then in the sight of God you are a sinner."

Where did I find these words to speak? I had not rehearsed them, and I did not make intentional use of them. They must have been expressions I had heard from Epaphras, or from Philemon or Luke, or Paul himself as he dictated his letters. They came to my mind as a river flows.

"Why should I be a sinner?" she protested. "I have done no wrong. I cannot be a sinner to a god of whom I have never heard!"

The fact of what she said was true. I was ignorant then. I did not know how to speak the word of God without helpless blundering.

"May I tell you?" I said.

"You have told enough. You should not have come here with your preaching. We are woodcutter people.

We have what we have been given. You will only bring us discontent."

She walked back slowly to the corner where the figures of the two household deities stood in their niche. She remained before them in silence, and I guessed that she was praying.

I was never more miserable than at that moment. I had failed so in what I tried to say.

After a time she spoke. "I told you that you were not like those of us in the trade of woodcutters. You cannot stay in this place. It will be better that you go."

I went to the doorway of the house. The two brothers and the older wife still worked on the beach. The stacks of salvaged timber had grown higher, and the group of neighbors searching along the shoreline had moved almost from sight.

"I will leave now."

"I am sorry," she said. "You have given me a shade of doubt, and I shall never escape from it. But I am glad that you came."

I turned back into the house, and walked over to her. I took her hand.

"I am glad for much," I said. "Yet I am sorry, too. This first time I have tried to explain about an existence so great that it lies beyond the greatness of the stars and the sun, I have failed."

I turned and went away.

XV

With nothing but the gifts of the clothing upon my back and the sandals upon my feet I left the house of the woodcutters. I walked through the forest and toward the highland away from the sea.

From that moment I was as a hunted beast, fearful of any eye that might perceive me. With no identification, no possessions, no story to tell, no destination, I was a derelict, empty and featureless, crawling through the countryside.

Of the days following I will say little. They were fearful times. Inland from the sea I found a great military road leading through the foothills from the south to the north. I know now that it was the Via Aurelia, the Roman highway which went all the way to the mountains above Italy. At the time I realized only that it must come out of Rome to the south. The road gave me a sense of direction.

My first glimpse of the Via Aurelia revealed also a long column of clanking legionaries moving north along it. I kept well hidden until they had passed, and then I proceeded forward only with extreme caution. I discovered soon that much traffic used the road, and that the highway was no place for me to be near.

I crossed it at night and hid myself among the barren hills beyond. I found springs, and did not lack water. Food was the great difficulty, for want of which I came near to starvation. At this time of year the hills provided almost nothing, and I was forced to approach the small farms in the flatlands.

In the hours of darkness I foraged among gardens, eating raw vegetables. Once I was able to steal a chicken.

From the beginning, I knew at heart that I had only one refuge, one possible place of survival. As I had felt the presence of Paul in the frightful hour of the shipwreck, so now I was drawn inevitably toward the city and the house on the Via Lata.

I could look for mercy nowhere else. The far-reaching laws of the Romans forced mercy out of any heart for those in my condition.

I became an apparition to bring terror, with matted beard and filth-stained clothing, sunken eyes and a bruised body. Not yet had human eyes set sight on me. Had that happened I would probably have been set upon and destroyed as a madman from the mountains. I found caves in the hills as I approached Rome, and I spent the daylight hours in hiding there. At last I crept into Rome itself by night on my hands and knees.

In the city I used the cellars of abandoned houses for hiding places, and once I hid in a crevice behind the manure pit of a stable. I reached the Tiber, but I dared not cross by a bridge, even in the blackness of night. With what must have been God-given strength I swam across the river in the face of the current flowing cold from the icy mountains. I was carried far downstream and lay exhausted on the farther bank until dawn. Through that day I hid shivering and wet in the mouth of a sewer.

How I finally came to the Via Lata I do not remember. Among the maze of dark streets I did at last find the familiar house, and still I had not been seen by any person. I came upon the door as I clutched against building walls, making of myself a flat shadow instead of a form.

To my dismay, I found that a soldier paced a beat before the house. His sword and armor gleamed in the starlight.

The soldier saw me, even as no more than a black and crouching shape.

"Who is there?" he demanded. "I ask, who is there? Answer!"

He approached.

"Mercy, in the name of God Jehovah," I croaked. "I take shelter in the house of Paul."

The guard hesitated. He came near and peered down at me with his sword held out.

"Are you man or beast?" he asked incredulously.

"Mercy, for Christ's sake," I managed to say.

"Oh." The guard drew back, and thought for a moment. "A Christian, I suppose," he grumbled.

At last he turned and pounded upon the door. The hour must have been toward morning, and all indoors were asleep. The soldier pounded longer.

After a time I heard the sound of chains beyond the door. A crack appeared, and a light shone out.

"There's someone here," the soldier said. "He seems nearly dead."

I staggered forward into the circle of light. I heard an exclamation, and a firm hand took me by the arm and led me through the door.

The one who took me in was Epaphras.

The shock to the Christians upon recognizing me ended their sleep that night. Luke the physician was called, and Tychicus also came to help. My clothes were removed. The frame of flesh and bones that remained of my body was washed, my slimy hair and beard were trimmed. I was given warm milk, and Luke stirred a medicine to ease the fever I had developed.

I was laid on a mattress to sleep, with a covering to keep me warm.

For most of that day I slept. Then, late, Epaphras came to talk, and to hear my story.

After he had listened to it all, he said, "You have acquired the faith of a Christian."

"I do not know," I said. "I have come here in desperation. That is not faith."

"Christ is a refuge for the desperate," he said.

"I had not faith enough to convince another person," I said.

"Perhaps you have discovered conviction within yourself," Epaphras replied. "I must take you to Paul. At this time he must know everything of you."

"I am putting him and all of you in this house into the greatest danger," I said. "You know the penalties."

After that, Paul received me in his room. He stood with his hands clasped behind his back. In height he was rather small than large, and his head was turning bald. In his beard there were gray streaks. At first one might not have discovered in him—standing motionless there in his room—a man out of the ordinary.

Yet from his face, through his eyes, and by the very way in which he stood, he sent out such vibrancy of personality that one paused in awe. Even before hearing his voice, anyone in the presence of this man would feel with every nerve the energy in his nature. No man could be for long before him without knowing that never in a lifetime could he be dismissed from mind.

After Epaphras showed me into the room and had vanished again outside the closed door, we were left alone. No soldier was there. The place was exactly as it had been when I worked there as a scribe. Everything was so much the same that I might never have left it at all.

The difference now lay in my feeling toward this man who belonged to God.

"Onesimus, the letter writer," Paul said to me. "You have returned."

"Yes, master."

I fell to my knees before him.

"Bow not to me," he said. "Bow and give thanks to your God in Heaven."

"You saved me from drowning in the sea."

He frowned. He had not been told what had happened, or as yet anything at all of me.

"Stand up," he ordered. "What would you have me do while you remain in this condition?"

I rose unsteadily to my feet.

"What is this you say about drowning?" he asked.

"My story is long. I beg that you may listen, for there is much also that I ask you to tell me—about myself."

"Indeed," he said, "I cannot know what should be told to you about yourself until I hear more concerning you." He raised up his head to look at me, for I was taller than he. "I watched you, Onesimus the useful one, when you sat writing into the letters the words I spoke aloud. I thought then that you were ready to believe in Christ, but you did not know it."

"I think that I am ready now, master," I said.

Paul shook his head. "Go, Onesimus, and kneel not to me but to God—by the open window, and look at the setting sun over the city. If you feel the hand of Christ upon you, you will talk."

I went to the window, and fell on my knees—not to Paul as I wished but before the open sky and to the setting sun.

I found there only a great emptiness.

Paul said, "You have come in search of Christ?"

"I believe so," I said. "Yet still I do not know."

Somehow I managed to tell him my story. I confessed that I was a fugitive from Philemon of Colossae. I told how I had met Epaphras long ago, first in Ephesus and then again at my master's house. I spoke of Mithra, and of the disillusionment that came after the death of Persilio. I spoke of Rome and of my sudden flight, of the shipwreck and my rescue, and of the days and nights of horror before I reached this house.

Paul did not interrupt. I finished and laid my head upon the sill of the window.

Soon I felt his hand upon my shoulder. "My son," he said, "some find faith easily; some by a hard road. You are of the last. Your road is the most hard." He paused, and then went on, "You are right to doubt yourself. You have not yet found your faith."

I longed to hear words of reassurance, and I lifted my head from the window sill. After my confession, I made myself believe that I had achieved a spiritual nobility satisfactory to this leader of the Christians.

"Christ is not found so soon with those who travel the hard road," Paul told me. "Be not deceived by false security along the way."

"But that night on the sea, did I not believe?"

"Perhaps," Paul said. "Faith has not remained with you. You are sorry only for the mishaps you have brought upon yourself. You regret the condition into which you were born, and from which you find no escape. You are glad for the salvation of your physical self in this house of refuge from a pursuing world. But you cannot fool yourself into believing that you have faith in Christ."

"Master, what can I do?"

He lifted his hand. I saw the sharp light in his eyes. "When you understand the suffering of all humanity, and not of yourself alone, you will be a more humble follower of our Lord. When you can share in the agony of Christ as well as your own, you will be ready."

I was greatly disheartened. I had expected comfort from Paul. I did not receive it.

"I think that we have spoken enough for this time," he said. "There will be more another time."

"Master," I said, "I am a fugitive from the law of the Romans."

"As long as my life be spared, I trust that my roof will protect those under it with the blessing of Jesus Christ. You will remain here, in safety." A smile crossed his face. "I shall welcome your help in writing my letters."

XVI

In the house of Paul I found sanctuary, and rest. The daily routine of the Christians was simple, although the activity of the household was intense. Morning began early with prayers and a light breakfast. The business of the day began at once, and it did not stop until the evening meal. Then there was time for meditation, and for the discussion of questions which might have arisen during the day.

Frequently in those evening hours I listened to the physician Luke, who had remarkable authority in the use of words. He told me many things that he had heard of Jesus Christ from the lips of Peter and other men who had been with Jesus during his ministry and at the time of his death. Luke intended to write an account of what he had heard, to preserve the truth of Christ's life.

Luke had accompanied Paul and Timothy on most of the apostle's journeys through Macedonia, Asia, Syria, and down to Tyre and Jerusalem. The physician kept records of the things he saw and heard on the journeys. He planned also to compile a narrative account of these, so that Christians might know of the acts of the apostles throughout the Roman Empire.

One had a feeling of urgency in Paul's house, as if time might stop at any moment and there was so much to be accomplished first. In spite of imprisonment within his home, Paul was free to carry on his ministry and his work with the Christians, and many people came every day to hear him speak in the large room of the house. I was glad to join in the work there as far as I was able, not only in writing letters but in copying manuscripts and taking notes from books. I believe that I can say that I was useful.

Now I also came to know John Mark, recently arrived in Rome from traveling, who also planned to set down Christ's life in writing. Each day Mark, Epaphras, Tychicus, and others of Paul's group went into the streets of Rome to carry abroad their word of Christ. They preached at meetings both in private homes and in public places. Wherever there was an ear to hear, the meaning of the gospel was told. The Christian congregation in Rome increased in numbers uncounted, including Hebrews and Gentiles alike, citizens and slaves, rich and poor, men and women from Nero's palace and from the market places.

The Christian faith was growing also beyond Rome and the shores of Italy. Reports came regularly of the activities of disciples. Letters from across the sea told how baptisms were steadily increasing under the ministries of local bishops.

Epaphras told me that some weeks before Paul had received unhappy rumors from Colossae. The church there appeared to be deviating from Christian principles of worship. News coming from the Phrygian city indicated that all the teachings of Epaphras had been forgotten. The congregation of Colossae was reported to be reverting to spurious mysticism, to the sacrifices of the old Oriental religions. The people were going back to Mithraism with the name of Jesus Christ merely substituted for Mithra. Some among the young men were adopting lives of asceticism and withdrawing from the company of other people. They retired into contemplation and inactivity, abandoning the company of men and women, and took joy in their own physical self-denials.

These things worried Paul. They violated precepts that he had set out for every church. Paul, Epaphras told me, believed that the life of a Christian should be one of humility and good work on earth, with the steadfast hope of redemption after death. To reject the normal affairs of the world only glorified false vanity. Paul was angered and disappointed by the waywardness of the Colossians. He had despatched an urgent request for further news from the Phrygian city, and he impatiently awaited the answer.

I could well understand what had happened. I remembered how Philemon's faith wavered with uncertainty, and how Archippus had taken to self-mortification. The Christians of Colossae had confused the old beliefs with the new. What I heard from Epaphras did not surprise me.

For a long time I dared not leave the house to appear in public. At last Epaphras persuaded me to go with him to a service of worship at the home of Calpurnius Rufus, a wealthy Roman citizen, where a congregation of Christians met each week. Epaphras assured me there could be no undue danger. Therefore, dressed in a tunic and mantle given to me by Aristarchus of the Christian household—Aristarchus being of my size—I went out. The winter day was cold and the sky overcast. But I breathed deeply of the outdoor air, being grateful for my changed condition since my crawling arrival at the house on the Via Lata. I had fully recovered health and strength, and the state of my mind had returned to calmness. I had gained a certain assurance at least under the canopy of Christian protection.

Epaphras and I walked in the direction of the Quirinal hill, where the house of Calpurnius Rufus was built against the slope and surrounded by a wall and gardens. Others were arriving, too, and servants led the way into the long hall of the mansion. Men and women already present waited with reverent attention and bowed heads for the service to begin.

Epaphras went forward to assist with the service and left me standing with the rest of the company. I found myself beside three men dressed in work clothing, probably slaves who had laid down their tools to come to the meeting. At my other hand was a perfumed woman of the court, who may have been borne there in her own litter. I could not help but notice that the faces of these four people held in common that expression of humility and awe which seemed usual with Christians when they felt that they were about to stand in the presence of their God.

Our host Calpurnius Rufus, clad simply and not in the usual toga of a citizen, began by offering a prayer. It was in the Hebrew form which Christ himself had directed his disciples to make use of each day, the one beginning with the words, *Our Father who art in Heaven. . . .*

After hearing this prayer each day in Paul's house, by now I knew the words, and I repeated them along with the rest. I thought of how few material gains this invocation of Jehovah requested. Only one phrase, *Give us this day our daily bread,* asked for a corporeal benefit. Excepting the requests for guidance from temptation, for deliverance from evil, and for forgiveness of sin, all the rest contained praise of God. How unlike the religions of Rome and the East, in which the gods were principally exhorted for worldly fortune and success!

Epaphras preached to the people, beginning with a message sent through him by Paul. He would have come to them, Paul said, were it not for his imprisonment. Yet whether he could come to them or not, he was with them in his thoughts. "Paul asks that you stand fast in one spirit," Epaphras said, "and strive together with one mind for the faith of the gospel. He makes his request to you, that in lowliness of mind each one shall esteem the other better than himself. Let every man look not only to his own things, but also to the well-being of others."

Epaphras continued by speaking of Christ's address from the mountain to the multitude. I listened carefully, for this was the first time I had heard these words of the gospel.

The blessings of God would fall on the meek, the lowly, the ones who thought not of themselves with pride and satisfaction. I was astonished at this strange idea. What of the rulers, the governors, the conquerors, the warriors? What of the rich, the heads of the state, the owners of slaves? What of Philemon? What indeed of this same Calpurnius Rufus, a wealthy man, in whose house I stood?

Were not those who had such privileges before blessed by God?

I looked at Calpurnius, and saw him clad in simple dress. I saw humility in his face, and I remembered that he shared his mansion with these worshippers.

Slowly I began to understand what humbleness before Jesus meant. Humbleness, and meekness, was of the spirit. The rich could be humble as well as the poor. Calpurnius was humble. I thought of the woodcutters by the sea and how in goodness they had shared with me their small portions. Perhaps, without knowing so, they were as much blessed by God as the wealthy Roman citizen.

I thought of myself, who had cherished dreams of wealth and treasure. I had envied my master. I had acted with ingratitude and pride, and had run away from Philemon out of revenge and hate. I had stolen, and I had lied. The burden of sin before God lay heavily upon me.

Forgive us our sins, as we forgive those who sin against us. This indeed was humility.

Epaphras finished speaking, and the group knelt again to pray. As we went onto our knees I noticed the upturned face of a girl a short distance in front of me.

May God forgive me at this later day, but at that moment all thought of religion vanished from my mind.

The girl was the one called Florentina, companion-slave of Aurelia. I recognized her from my one visit to the apartment of Octavia, the wife of Caesar.

My heart beat fast, and a door opened once more, it seemed, revealing a vista which I had thought to be shut away forever.

I had thought of Aurelia so often, especially during the horrible journey from the seacoast into Rome, and then again during my subsequent period of recovery. But the human spirit can be numbed into final submission. By so many obviously hopeless obstacles, my normal feelings had been crushed at last. Partly through physical exhaustion, I suppose, and partly because of the knowledge of my own desperate position, Aurelia had become less important than the basic necessity of survival on earth.

Only on this day, when I dared to go out on the streets with Epaphras, had I recovered my normal spirits.

So I was ripe for news again of Aurelia. The chance presence of the serving girl Florentina made it possible.

The prayers which closed the service of worship went unheard past my ears. I watched Florentina as she knelt, fearful that she might after all vanish away if I ceased staring for even a moment. She was dressed in a simple and becoming mantle, and a hood covered her hair. Nothing about her showed that she was so close to the wife of Caesar. She remained very still during the prayers. It was certain that her devotion ran deep.

At the instant the service was concluded, I hurried to

her side. Many people were standing together in conversation, and I could speak to the girl without attracting attention.

I touched her elbow. She turned quickly, her demure face startled.

"Please, you will pardon me for coming to you at this time," I said swiftly. "You are the one called Florentina, serving the wife of Caesar?"

She was strangely alarmed.

"Yes," she replied. She did not recognize me at all.

"I would have you carry a message to Aurelia," I said. "In secret, for the sake of all that you hold dear."

Her eyes grew round. "To Aurelia?"

"Tell her that you have met the one who carried jewels to Octavia one evening some time ago."

She stepped back involuntarily. "Oh. . . ."

"And tell Aurelia that I must see her! Tell her. . . ."

Florentina shook her head. "Now I remember. You are the one of whom I spoke afterward to her. Aurelia was much disturbed by your visit to Octavia."

"Tell her that I am in Rome and that I must talk with her."

"I cannot. It could only bring trouble."

"No!" I said desperately. "Through no one but you is this possible. I beg of you, give her my message."

She hesitated. "If I did speak to her, of what use would it be? She will not see you."

"You do not know that."

"She wished that she had not seen you that one time. Aurelia told me nothing, but I could guess that you were the bearer of danger—not only for us, but perhaps even for our mistress."

"If that be true, then it is also true that Aurelia knows who I am. She will remember an afternoon by the sea. You will tell her that, for her own sake!"

Florentina was upset. "Because you are here—I suppose because we are both here together—I will tell

Aurelia. It is against my wish to do so. But she will not see you."

"You are Christian. Bring her here for the service next week," I urged. "She will come."

"Aurelia is not a Christian," Florentina said, shaking her head.

"Does it matter? She can make it a reason to come. Tell her—I will meet her in the garden outside the house."

At that moment Epaphras came up to us. He nodded greetings to Florentina.

"My salutations," he said. "It is good that you are with us again."

"I would not be elsewhere," she replied, "as long as my mistress gives me liberty to come."

"And is all well in the household of the Emperor?" Epaphras asked.

She looked shyly down at the floor. "We do not know of Caesar's household," she said. "We are apart from there." She glanced up again. "I have spoken more of Christ to my mistress during the week. She listens to what I say, and is much impressed and comforted."

"Perhaps she will yet become Christian!" Epaphras said. "The wife of Caesar. . . ."

"No!" Florentina said quickly. "Octavia has already told me that she will not change. She lives in danger enough, and if she came here she would be followed. She fears the result to all concerned with this church."

"Then I will go to her apartment," Epaphras said. "Arrange a time for me. . . ."

Florentina put out her hand. "Not now," she said. "You do not know how we live. It is enough for her to allow me to come here. Yet I will tell her of your sermon today."

Epaphras bowed his head. "Florentina, I am sure you will repeat it better than I have said it."

"I could not be so worthy," she told him. "Good-bye."

She did not look at me again. With light steps she withdrew and went from the house. She had pulled her hood close over her forehead.

I could trust that my message would be delivered.

Epaphras looked at me quizzically. "She is one of the most faithful," he said. "You have met her before?"

"In a way," I replied evasively. "I have asked her to deliver a message. Next week she will bring the answer."

I smiled with confidence. The joy within me permitted no thought that Aurelia would not come.

"I am suspicious of you," Epaphras said. His eyes twinkled. "I will ask no more—but be cautious that you tempt not disaster."

"I am cautious," I said.

XVII

I have told of my work for Paul during this time of residence in his house.

From the beginning I wrote letters for him at his dictation, as I had when I was employed by the publisher Barea. Each morning I went to the apostle's room and took my place by the window. Pen in hand, I waited while the pale winter sun cast its light across the yard behind the house.

Some days Paul sat in dark silence with his thoughts, until all at once he would begin to speak at great speed. Then I would be pushed beyond measure to record his words. At other times he would be affable and congenial, dictating with consideration for the pace of my pen.

He did not say anything more to me concerning myself, but accepted me as one of the associates with him in his home of imprisonment. He was aware of my presence around the house during each day—at meal times, in the services of worship which I attended because it was expected of me, and when passing from room to room. Always he nodded cordially.

Paul had helped to make it easy for me to shut my eyes to the future. He did not question the length of my stay, or mention the dangers inherent in my presence in the house.

Perhaps he did not press me because he knew nothing of his own future. In the cheerful and congenial air of that house, I for one could scarcely comprehend the cloud that hung over its occupants. Paul was in fearful danger of his life, for always his enemies pressed the government to destroy him. When the day might come for his trial, no one could guess. Meanwhile time dragged on. Paul's serenity in the face of possible death continually surprised me. He was not concerned in the least for his own person, but only for the continuance of the work which he did for Christ.

He did not underestimate his task. He believed that he was a minister for God under a mandate received from Christ himself. His responsibility was to build what he called the living church of God. Through him Christianity was transformed from a division of heresy of the Hebrew faith into a new, enthusiastic religion founded on Christ as the Son of God.

The imprisonment of Paul in Rome was a subject of much public interest. His fate was a cause of conjecture throughout the Empire, for he was a man of considerable renown, not only because of his standing as a citizen but on account of his great work in establishing Christian churches. The apostle was grateful that news about himself had traveled so far. For better or for worse, he believed, his captivity caused talk. Christianity would become more widely known. Whether he lived or died, Paul was convinced that the churches of Christ would benefit.

When Paul dictated to me, I listened carefully. I sincerely wished to acquire Christian faith. Earnestly I tried to discover the key which would unlock my heart, and I brought to the subject all the interest of my inquiring mind. For a long time I remained unable to feel the impact of this faith with anything but dispassionate concern.

Then, on the morning after my meeting with Florentina, the moment did come. It was like a sudden bright flash of great understanding, or perhaps like a vision, a miraculous unveiling of infinite splendor.

Although I had been prepared for it, I did not expect it at that time or in the way that it came. I had slept little through the night and was too breathless to eat, for the prospect of seeing Aurelia carried me on a joyous wave of excitement. She occupied all my thoughts. My footsteps were light, and I felt dizzy with anticipation. Spiritual matters were far from my mind.

Restlessly, I went earlier than usual to work in Paul's room. I was at his door, pen in hand, a half hour before the appointed time. I entered the room quietly, as I always did, and closed the door gently behind me.

Then I saw Paul on his knees at the window. His face was turned upward and his hands reached out to the sky.

He was not praying in the ordinary manner. His body trembled; his outstretched arms were taut. Every muscle vibrated with tension, of anxiety or earnestness. His fingers bent in supplication, and even the hairs of his beard shook.

I pressed back silently against the closed door, wishing that I were not there. I realized that I had intruded upon a private communion. I remained as still as possible, breathing softly.

If Paul had heard me come in, he gave no indication.

He prayed in a whisper too low for words to be distinguishable. Then all at once the apostle cried out with a loud voice in the Hebrew language: "Oh, thou living God Jehovah in heaven, give me strength—give me strength in my hours—"

The cry was so unexpected that my heart leapt. Then Paul hid his face in his hands. His head bowed low; all the tautness of muscle went from him.

I heard Paul the apostle sob as he knelt at the window.

My flesh tingled, and my eyes must have widened as I witnessed what was happening. For Paul—the strong, the unconquerable, the wise and understanding—to come to tears was unbelievable.

Slowly Paul raised his head. Then he said without turning, "Onesimus, my son, will you come to pray with me?"

"Yes, master."

I crossed the room step by step, almost reluctantly. I knelt beside him at the window, without wanting to do so.

"Yesterday I received a letter from Archippus of Colossae," Paul said slowly.

I glanced at the apostle. He was apt to say startling things at unexpected moments.

"The Christians of that church have been led astray by false philosophy and vain deceit," he said. "The wrath of God shall come upon the children of disobedience. They who do wrong shall receive for the wrongs they do."

Paul covered his face with his hands.

"I wish that my time of waiting would be over," he said in a tone of great weariness. "Often I think that I do not know which I would choose: to depart this life and to be at last with Christ, or to continue my work here where I know that I am needed." He paused, and then he said, "I have so little strength remaining, my son, and so little time."

I looked at Paul again as I knelt at his side. Why did he say these things to me?

Tears were on the apostle's face. What could I say to him? The people of Colossae had disappointed and disillusioned him. After all his work, all his devotion to his ministry of Christ, Paul had discovered that the faithful could lose their faith, that believers might no longer believe.

And he was helpless, confined to his house in Rome while troubled cities throughout the Empire longed to hear his reassuring words.

Who but God could know how far or how near was the end for him? Death sentences for Roman citizens by custom were meted out with the dignity of the headsman's block, rather than crucifixion or contests in the games arena which ended the lives of less privileged criminals. I could myself imagine a flashing sword poised in air, while the head of Paul bent beneath. Surely, in the dark of night, Paul must think these thoughts.

Part of a letter which he had dictated to me came back into my memory: So *if there is any encouragement in Christ, any incentive of love, any participation in the Spirit, any affection and sympathy, complete my joy by being of the same mind, having the same love, being in full accord and of one mind.*

That was Paul, the man himself, speaking in the wholeness of his hopes for all mankind. It was as noble an expression of life's motive as any man could utter.

But where God can succeed, every man in his deepest purpose must fail.

In that moment I was thinking with the utmost clarity, understanding what I had never understood before.

"It is not I who live, but Christ who lives in me," Paul said as if I had spoken aloud. "I am made a minister of God, to fulfill the word of God, the mystery which is Christ in you, the hope of glory."

The apostle's voice vibrated in depth so that it seemed to me he was not speaking in a small room held within four walls but out in the great spaces of the world and sky. I remember that I was looking then above the sunny courtyard toward the white clouds and the intense blue of the heavens. *Christ in you, the hope of glory.* . . . I had been considering Jesus as a man who walked the earth as Paul walked it, saying marvelous things and performing great miracles—but in the way that even Paul could do. I had thought of him as a man who died as men must die, as Paul himself might shortly die. But Paul had said, *It is not I who live, but Christ who lives in me.*

Could Christ live on in me as well, miserable as I was, when I had not faith in him? All at once the confusing pieces fell together into a whole, and I understood.

Jesus Christ had lived and died for faith in me, even the least of all mankind. It was not my faith so long sought which now I found, but Christ's faith for me.

Did I have a vision at that moment? I cannot say for certain. I do know that I felt a presence standing before me, within me. I heard a voice—or in my mind I did— which said, "Onesimus, follow me." This voice I had never heard before. I could not have disobeyed.

Now I can write with the calmness of faith. Faith lies beyond comprehension and reasoning. Once something comes within reason, it is no longer of faith but of substance.

Sorry is the plight of the man who has no faith. I, Onesimus, know of that which I speak.

I rose to my feet that morning, overwhelmed by a great and puzzling emotion.

Paul had risen and stood in the center of the room. As I turned, he said, "And there appeared unto him a cloven tongue of fire, and sat upon him, and he was filled with the Holy Ghost."

I caught my breath. Luke had once told me of the coming of the Holy Spirit to the disciples in Jerusalem. I had felt it myself. And Paul knew that it had happened.

"The peace of God be with you, Onesimus my son," Paul said. He put his hands on my shoulders. "This day you will be baptized in the name of Jesus Christ."

I write these things as they happened to me. I speak not for others.

Timothy came into the room then, and on that same morning was begun the dictation of a letter to the church at Colossae. Paul was again a man of force and strength. Why have I written of his fears and doubts? All is over now. May I be forgiven if I have shown that even this strongest of men also had the weakness of humankind. No man can stand alone. The need for God is universal.

The letter to the people of Colossae was started: *Paul, an apostle of Christ Jesus by the will of God, and Timothy our brother, to the saints and faithful brethren in Christ at Colossae: Grace to you and peace from God our Father. . . .*

XVIII

At the end of a week came the day when I would meet Aurelia. I returned to the house of Calpurnius Rufus with far different feelings than those I had when I sent the urgent message through the girl Florentina.

Now I had a gift to share with her, the possession of Christian faith. I longed to tell her of the miracle that had happened to me, to communicate to her the uplifting experience, to make her see as I saw.

This time I went alone at the hour for the service of worship. I passed without difficulty through the gate of the house and waited outside under the trees of the garden. I watched as people came for the devotions by ones and twos and threes, all passing on into the house with a quiet and reverent manner. I prayed that one day Aurelia would go with me, hand in hand, to worship God. Even as I prayed, I felt the conviction that this time would come.

During the week before I had not thought for a moment that Aurelia would not heed my message. Perhaps I counted too much on my expectations, for Florentina had warned me. At the beginning I assumed too much in believing that she would want to speak with me again. Perhaps I had created for myself an illusion of love.

The egotism which had directed so much of my life had to be counted among the number of sins which still lay as a burden on my heart. That same egotism had made me insistent in my demand upon Florentina when I so unexpectedly met her.

Yet I waited more anxiously as time went on and neither Florentina nor Aurelia appeared. The servants of Calpurnius glanced at me curiously. Inside the house the service was about to begin.

Then Florentina entered quickly through the gate, and paused. The hood was drawn tightly over her head.

Aurelia followed her! She hesitated, and Florentina hurried up the path toward the house.

My joy burst all limits. I hurried forward, forgetting, of course, how all persons may change in the course of time and circumstance. In Ephesus I had been a youth of sixteen, not much more than a boy unbearded and lanky. Now I was in my early twenties, grown taller and broader. Since coming to the house of Paul, I had retained a small, cropped beard. My face surely showed the travails through which I had been. The one whom Aurelia saw waiting for her must have been a stranger.

She herself had not changed. Her beauty was the same—without flaw. She was if possible more perfect, more aglow with a mysterious light like some fine jewel. She wore a plain mantle similar to Florentina's, and she kept her face shrouded by a hood.

"Aurelia!" I cried.

She shrank back slightly.

"You asked me to come," she said. "I do not know why."

"I must talk with you," I told her. "There is so much for us to say to one another. Let us walk this way."

I led her from the servants' hearing across the dry winter grass. She came at my side with eyes downcast.

"I am glad to see you," I said. Words were suddenly hard to find. "Have you been well, Aurelia?"

"Very well, I am cared for, and content."

"What strange chance, to think that I found your friend here last week!"

"What you call strange, I think I should call unfortunate."

"Aurelia, no! Fate has brought us together again."

She shook her head. "Not fate, but folly. I should not have come today."

"I was certain that you would."

"Why did you send for me?" she asked. "It can lead to nothing."

"When I tell you all that I have to say, you will know that is not so."

"It is dangerous for you. Perhaps I have been followed. Perhaps even now they watch me. Octavia herself is always watched."

"It is not danger to me that I think about," I told her, "but to you. Yet in this place we are safe."

We had walked into the shadows under the palm trees near the garden wall. We were out of sight even from the house windows. In a small formal clearing among the shrubbery we found a place where we could stand without fear.

"Onesimus," she asked, troubled, "is it true that you deserted your master?"

"I left Philemon, if that is what you mean."

"Then you are a fugitive. I guessed as much when you came so foolishly to my mistress. I guessed also that you had stolen those jewels from your master."

"It was a great sin, Aurelia," I admitted, "but there was no other way."

"So," she said, raising her gaze to meet mine. "You are not only a runaway slave, but also a thief who has stolen from the hand that sheltered you. You have broken the laws of the Romans. You have dared to sell contraband property to the wife of the Emperor."

Her words hurt. I knew Aurelia's standards of loyalty, and I was much ashamed to appear so base in her eyes. I could deny nothing.

"I suppose I could add even more if I told all," I said miserably. "Aurelia, what I did was mostly in the hope of finding you."

"That is not true. You are only excusing yourself."

"It has been a long time and a hard road from Colossae to this garden. Please understand, Aurelia, in these few minutes. . . ."

"I would rather have been left with the memories of you, which I held dear, than to know now these things that you have done."

I reached out eagerly to take her hands.

"Then you have memories? You have not forgotten?"

She whispered, "Do you suppose if I had forgotten I would have come here today?"

"Aurelia, my beloved!"

I looked into those dark eyes which I had once called blue pools. Aurelia smiled, but even smiling she shook her head.

"No, Onesimus, whom I did love," she said. "We must understand that we have nothing. We are no more free for each other in Rome than we were in Ephesus."

"Wait, we have more than you think. We can have hope and love and life for all eternity. I must tell you that I have become a Christian."

"I supposed as much when I heard where you had met Florentina."

"But last week I was no Christian! It happened between then and now."

Aurelia looked at me with astonishment.

"Would you have sent for me last week had you been a Christian then?"

"Yes! Even more emphatically than I did. I can say now that which I would not have known to say then. Together we can have hope—through faith. We can share the worship of God. We will pray together, and our future will be bright after all."

"You believe that praying would make all this come true?"

I detected scorn in her voice.

"Yes, I do believe. I will ask Paul to pray for us, too."

"You can guess what he would say about me."

"Everyone is welcome to come to Christ, Aurelia."

"Well, not even Vesta herself could change what is destined for us. Let us not make fools of ourselves in this way."

"You must listen. . . ."

"I have heard enough of these Christian beliefs from Florentina," she replied. "It cannot help."

"Come now to the service going on in the house. I will show you that Christ *can* hear even us. . . ."

"Your Christ cannot make of you any more than a fugitive slave! He cannot release you from bondage to your master in Colossae, or set me free from my mistress."

"My master is God Jehovah," I said.

"You think that you can forget your first master?" she demanded. "The law of the Romans does not permit you to change so easily."

"Can you not understand?" I begged her. "God in heaven is master of all men."

"The one who owns a slave is his master," Aurelia replied. "I am owned by Octavia. I have no right which belongs to me. You, Onesimus, have no right of your own on earth either."

I was about to dispute further with her, to claim my right to my soul even if I could not to my body. But suddenly the words would not come. If Christ were master only of my soul, then indeed I was beholden to two masters—and for earthly things Philemon had prior claim.

Confusion fell upon me. I was at a loss to understand this new puzzle.

"No," Aurelia said sadly. "There is so much that cannot be. Our destinies are fixed, Onesimus. You remember I said it long ago?"

"Destinies need not be fixed! I changed mine when I left Philemon."

"You did not change it. It is still the same. You have merely changed your state to that of a hunted one, under a burden of sin."

"Christ forgives sins!"

"And Philemon?" she asked.

I could not make any answer.

"Does that not prove the master?" she said gently. "You ask me to believe in Christ, who forgives sins. But in your present state, is not Philemon the stronger?"

Suddenly something burst upon my mind, so awful and frightening that sweat broke out upon me.

Aurelia cried in alarm. "What is it, Onesimus?"

"I see—one way—one way that might change my destiny. Would you believe, Aurelia, if it were so?"

"If it were so," she said. "What way is this?"

"I cannot tell—not now."

"Onesimus, I wish. . . ." Aurelia raised her hand, then let it down again. "Perhaps, once, I can come here again. But only once. Anything more might bring disaster. Good-bye."

She was gone, leaving only a trace of perfume in the air to remind me that she had been there.

"Aurelia!" I cried. "Aurelia, come back! I will tell you . . . !"

There were voices in the distance. The service in the house of Calpurnius was over. I saw Florentina hurrying through the gate.

"Oh, God!" I said aloud. "Guide me in this hour to do thy will!"

XIX

"Timothy and I have determined to send this letter to the Colossian church—direct by the hand of Tychicus."

All night after meeting Aurelia in the garden, I had suffered tortures in my mind. Now what Paul said reached my ears as a thunderclap. It caught me as a blow that took the breath from my body. I shook as from the ague.

Paul had been pacing the floor of his room, dictating during the morning more of the letter to Colossae. Against the far wall, Timothy sat at the foot of the couch, sometimes interrupting with a suggestion. I was at the writing desk by the window.

To bring to the people of Colossae a more responsible interpretation of the Christian faith had become the key of Paul's present work. Much had been done on the letter in this direction, and much careful planning had gone into it.

But the apostle's sudden announcement that Tychicus was to take the letter in person to Colossae caught me without warning.

After he had said this, the apostle stopped his pacing. I knew that he was looking at me.

No sound came from Timothy.

I heard a bird sing out in the courtyard. Noises of the city reached my ears: the cries of hawkers, the rumble of a cart. Someone in the house called. Routine sounds at this moment became vastly important, as if I could clutch in my desperation at the normal objects they represented.

Slowly I was compelled to look up from the manuscript on the table. I met Paul's gaze.

"Why are you so afraid of what I have said?" he asked.

My lips moved without speech. Then I replied, "I know what you would have me do."

"If you know what I would have you do before I say it, then you must already have thought it yourself."

"Yes, master, I have."

"Then it is not what I would have you do. It is what you would do."

I laid my head upon the desk. I had known since meeting Aurelia in the garden of Calpurnius.

The human flesh is known to be weak, and the spirits of men inevitably stumble. Of mankind, I have been in my time the weakest. I could not confront alone this fearful choice. Paul's intention to send Tychicus with the letter settled it.

I must return to Philemon.

My master might forgive, in the spirit of Christ. The choice for him would be hard if he did. What I had done would call upon my head the vengeance of all slave owners for the sakes of their properties. I ought to become a lesson to transgressors, an example to other slaves. I faced torture, ignominy, and death under frightful circumstances.

Now that I had found life, I should lose it.

Paul crossed to me and laid his hand upon my shoulder. "Would you perpetuate a sin, my son?" he asked.

"You do not know—an escaped slave . . . a thief . . . the torture. . . ." My protest faded in my throat. I saw the sorrow deep in Paul's eyes. I remembered the death that he too faced. I thought of the tortures which he had endured.

"I am sorry," I said miserably. "I had forgotten."

"You have put away the other man which was yourself, and through baptism you have been born again as a new man. The other man is dead, and with him his sins. The new man lives in the Spirit. Walk no longer where the other man walked."

I looked at Paul. "I understand," I said, "but yet I am afraid!"

"There is no fear when one walks in the new way of Christ."

I swallowed hard. Through the window I saw the sunlight. Out under the sky was freedom—life. What price did I pay for Christian belief?

At that instant Timothy left the couch and also came to me.

"Onesimus," he said, "I have known you these days. I have seen you, and I believe I have understood you. The past lies upon you as a liability, so that you cannot move about for the burden of it. To discharge that liability means that you may gain an asset even greater."

"How?" I asked, not believing.

"You will not only lift off your burden, but you will rise in grace as if on wings," Timothy said. "Do you not see that to sin and then confess may perhaps bring the greater reward than not to sin at all? The first road is harder than the second road."

I lifted my head. "I suppose so," I replied.

Paul stood at the window now, his hands clasped behind his back. Timothy waited.

I said, "I will go to my master in Colossae."

"You go in Christ, and Christ is with you," Timothy said.

"I must tell you more," I said with difficulty. "There is one in Rome named Aurelia. I may not see her again."

Timothy asked, "What would you wish?"

"She is slave to Octavia, wife of Nero. She serves with Florentina, who has become a Christian in the congregation of Calpurnius. I hold her in honor—and love. Would that I could take her for wife."

"How could that be possible?" Timothy asked again, this time with astonishment.

"It is not possible," I said. "We are slaves, to our masters on earth. But I believe that Aurelia would hear the Word of God."

All this time Paul had not moved.

"We will do what we can," Timothy said. "The palace of Nero is hard to approach."

Then Paul said to me, "You have become beloved of us, my son. Timothy, you will ask the girl Aurelia to come here. I would speak with her."

Then the apostle said to me, "I have already talked with Timothy concerning your master in Colossae. We will give to you a letter which you are to deliver into the hand of Philemon. We will suggest to him that in Christian spirit he will forgive and pardon you." Paul's eyes looked deeply into mine. "I cannot ask directly, but I may hope that he will send you back to me in Rome, that you might continue your work with us."

I could not see Aurelia, or Florentina either. The Christian girl did not appear the next week at the house of Calpurnius. Those in Octavia's apartment were under strict surveillance by Caesar's orders.

The rumors in Rome disturbed me greatly. Poppaea, the mistress of Nero, wished to be his wife in place of Octavia. Yet the population of the city loved Octavia, who by her nature had endeared herself to the people. Even Caesar dared not risk the wrath of the Romans by the unreasonable putting aside of his lawful wife. What might come, no one could guess.

I had no time to find out more, for the letter to the congregation of Colossae was nearly completed. Paul spent all his energies upon it, while Tychicus made preparations to set forth from Rome.

What Paul said in his letter is not for me to include in my account here. I write only of my own struggle to-

ward faith. But certain words of Paul wrought deeply in
my heart, so that each day I became more changed. I
grew in strength of mind, and I was the more prepared
for what I had to do.

Paul admonished the Colossians to forsake their previous devotions to false deities and practices. He had
been told of the divisions in their ranks, causing dissension and bitterness between neighbors and even among
families: *Put on then, as God's chosen ones, holy and
beloved, compassion, kindness, lowliness, meekness,
and patience; forbearing one another, if one has a complaint against another, forgiving each other; as the Lord
has forgiven you, so you also must forgive.*

And to the families of Colossae, Paul said: *Wives, be
subject to your husbands, as is fitting in the Lord. Husbands, love your wives, and do not be harsh with them.
Children, obey your parents in everything, for this
pleases the Lord. Fathers, do not provoke your children, lest they become discouraged.*

Then Paul wrote: *Slaves, obey in everything those
who are your earthly masters, not with eyeservice as
menpleasers, but in singleness of heart, fearing the
Lord. Whatever your task, work heartily as serving the
Lord and not men, knowing that from the Lord you will
receive the inheritance as your reward; you are serving
the Lord Christ.*

I could not fail to respond with my whole nature to
this command. The message I took for my personal use,
and I knew that I could carry it on to my fellow slaves
of the household of Philemon, advising them certainly
as no one else could do.

The letter came to its end: *Tychicus will tell you all
about my affairs; he is a beloved brother and faithful
minister and fellow servant in the Lord. I have sent him
to you for this very purpose, that you might know how
we are and that he may encourage your hearts, and with
him Onesimus, the faithful and beloved brother who is*

*one of yourselves. They will tell you of everything that
has taken place here.*

What had I done to deserve Paul's words, which lifted me to be one with all who worshipped Christ? I knew not my worthiness, and believe it not even now. The greater is the miracle of Paul's trust in me.

Epaphras sent his greetings in the letter, and Luke did, and the others of Paul's household. So it was finished with an instruction that it be read also by the church at Laodicea—and with one other personal instruction:

And say to Archippus, "See that you fulfill the ministry which you have received in the Lord."

Paul signed the letter in his own hand: *Remember my fetters. Grace be with you.*

The day came for Tychicus and me to take leave of Paul and the others in his house.

I had heard no more of Aurelia. I left with only the comfort of Timothy's assurance that word of my departure would go to her at the earliest opportunity.

Timothy worked with Paul on the writing of the letter to Philemon which I was to bear, as it was not to be in my own handwriting. At the last moment, the apostle handed it to me, unsealed.

"Master," I said, "I would ask that you seal it, that Philemon will know I give it to him fresh and unspoiled. I would rather present myself to him on my own account, without my own awareness of what you have written on my behalf."

Paul nodded. "It is better so," he said. "So be it."

He sealed the letter himself.

Then the apostle embraced me, and Tychicus. "May God be with you both," he said.

"And with you," I said.

He went from us quickly. We left the house, knowing nothing of the future for ourselves or for those whom we left in Rome.

But as we began our journey down the Appian Road for Puteoli and the sea, I felt the greatest joy in my own heart. Already the burden of the past was dropping from my shoulders, and I traveled as if I flew.

XX

The dry, hot hills led up to the familiar gorge of the river Lycus, beyond which lay Colossae.

Here on the road I stopped Tychicus.

"You will go on without me," I said. "I will follow, for we ought not to enter the city together in case I am recognized and the soldiers apprehend us both."

"I will not fear," he said. "We will enter together as we have come together this far."

My urging was to no avail. We were riding ponies which we had bought in Ephesus after leaving our ship. The journey from Rome had seemed interminable, but we had survived storms and perils. Tychicus had been a constant shield to prevent my being questioned. But now the risk was greatest.

I wished only to reach the villa of Philemon without being first taken up on the streets.

We rode on, and all the way was familiar and unchanged. At last we came to the city wall and passed the gate.

"Now we will part," I insisted. "I will not have you share what well might happen to me. You will come later to the villa of Philemon?"

"Yes," he agreed. Tychicus had already decided to take lodgings at an inn, in response to my request that I face my master alone. Later, I was certain, Philemon would insist that Tychicus stay as guest in the household.

"Christ protect you," Tychicus said in farewell. "I will pray for your safety."

I held back my pony until Tychicus had moved on. Then I turned a corner. Shopkeepers were selling their wares, camels moved slowly with their burdens, and the narrow streets were filled with people as they had always been. I remembered so well these things which I had seen as a boy.

With what strange feelings I made my way toward that house which had been my home! I felt no doubts, and no fears in anticipation of the lash I must expect, or the ripping of tendons on the rack. I wondered only if old Zalgrebbo would still be in charge. I hoped that now I could hold my head high in his face.

Streaked with the stains of travel as I was, no one recognized me as Onesimus, the fugitive. I came up to the villa and opened the gate myself.

No servant appeared, and I did not ring the call bell. The hour approached noon. I felt certain that Philemon would be in the room that served for his business purposes.

Slowly I walked through the halls until I came to my master's room. A rush mat screened the doorway. I parted it, and stood inside.

Philemon was at his writing desk, reading from records that lay before him. His hair may have grayed somewhat, but in all other respects he was the same.

"Master," I said in a low voice.

Philemon looked up.

"Master, I have come," I said.

I waited, feeling my heart beating loudly in my chest like thunder.

He stared as if I had returned from the other side of death. His eyes narrowed, and his hands clenched until the knuckles were white. For a moment I wondered if he still thought of me as having been killed by bandits. He had no such impression in his mind.

He rose up to his feet as if he were about to spring. Without thinking I took a step backward.

"Dog!" Philemon began in a voice low and bitter. "That you should dare return to this house on which you spat with a snake's venom! That you should dare present your loathsome face in my presence!"

"I come to ask forgiveness, my master."

"So you found that your vile bravado and my stolen wealth are not enough! You come cringing back to escape the justice of the world. . . ."

"I do not cringe, my master," I said. "All that you say is true, except that I do not return to escape justice."

"You will not escape it here, I promise!" Philemon's voice rose to the roar of a lion. He turned to pull a bell cord at his side, and at the same time shouting, "Bring me Archippus! Archippus at once—and Zalgrebbo!"

I came further into the room. Of all the rages in which I had seen the master, none could equal this. His face had turned very dark and his eyes flamed. I had an idea that he might try to tear me apart with his own hands.

"You whom I trusted, whom I called my son, whom I fed and clothed—*you* who turned viper in my side, a jackal at my throat, a dog at my loins, *you* who dare to show yourself even in my house! Better you had cast yourself into the Lycus as you so deceitfully made out that robbers had cast you! Better for you if the bandits had stretched you cold in the sand! Better any fate than what will befall you now, with your presumption in returning again to this household!"

He came toward me, his head thrust forward. I tried to keep myself from flinching. Here was my punishment for the evil I had done; here the reward——

It happened quickly. Philemon was a strong man. The flat of his hand struck my left cheek, and I staggered. His other hand on the right cheek snapped my head on my neck like a whip. My skull seemed to burst. Blood spurted from my nose and mouth. I fell. . . .

I remember the sharp, biting cut of the lash across my shoulders that brought me to my senses. I looked up to see Zalgrebbo standing over me, and then again closed my eyes from the whip that cut across my face and body. If I screamed, I do not know. The pain went beyond knowing. Again and again the lash fell.

All the time I knew that it must be. I had to return to Colossae to receive this.

The beating stopped, but the pain did not. A voice wavered in my ears—"Onesimus! This is Onesimus?" The voice seemed familiar.

Someone knelt beside me. "So you came back? Where have you been all this time?"

The voice was that of Archippus.

I could not reply. I was gasping desperately for breath.

"Water," Archippus said, "bring water."

I felt the cold dash of a jugful of water across my face. It made me understand more clearly. I managed to open my eyes.

Archippus was on his knee, looking at me. Philemon spoke in the background.

"Here is meat for you, Zalgrebbo," Philemon said harshly. "Carrion for the crows to feed upon!"

"Where have you been?" Archippus repeated. "Where have you been?"

I managed to mutter the word, "Rome."

It was loud enough for Philemon to hear. "The lions of Caesar must have been asleep!" he said.

"Then who brought you back?" Archippus asked. "Soldiers?"

"I came of my own will."

Through my retching pain, I felt a sublime joy. The burden of my guilt had passed from me. The past was over!

Archippus stood up. "I do not understand this," he said. "You know the penalties for what you have done?"

"Yes."

"You will know them far better," Philemon shouted. "Zalgrebbo, take this man."

But Archippus lifted a hand in doubt. And at that moment the curtain at the doorway parted, and Apphia rushed into the room.

"Do I hear . . . !" she cried. "Onesimus, is it you? You really live!"

I could not raise my head, or look, for the terrible pain came again. I heard Philemon's anger turning more savage.

"Apphia!" he cried. "What do you do here? Leave this room! You know that women do not interfere with the slaves of a household!"

"Philemon, my husband," she answered, "have you forgotten that this is Onesimus, whom we likened to our son? He has returned to us, and what have you done?"

"I have ordered that he be pulled to pieces on the rack!"

"Yet I do not understand," Archippus said, still looking down at me. "Onesimus, why did you return?"

I suppose that I could have said then that I had become a Christian, that I had been sent by Paul the apostle to make amends to a Christian household. I did not. Something held me to the knowledge that I had to pay the penalty on my own account, not in pride but in true humility, knowing that if I did win a sincere measure of pardon from Philemon, it could be in no other way but this.

I whispered as best I could through bloody lips, "I have asked my master for forgiveness."

Philemon came toward me again. "Forgiveness!" he said between his teeth.

"Philemon!" Apphia clutched his arm. "Are you so free from blame that you need not ask forgiveness from God for your own sins?"

"Nor have I treated God as this man has treated me!"

"Father." Archippus too restrained him. "We should know more about this. I do not yet understand why Onesimus—if he is telling the truth—has come from Rome to Colossae to ask your forgiveness. Such a trip is long and costly. He seems not ill-fed or ill-dressed. If soldiers did not bring him—then what has brought him here?"

Again I could have made answer.

I repeated, "I confess my faults. I ask my master to forgive what I have done."

"Under the law you may die," Archippus told me. "You have not said where you received the money for this trip. Did you steal again?"

I shook my head in denial.

"Wait!" Apphia exclaimed. "Have we in this house so far forgotten the spirit of Jesus Christ? I knew that we had gone far from what we learned of Paul and Epaphras. I did not know we had gone as far as this! Where, oh my husband, is God's mercy in *your* heart?"

Philemon paused. He frowned.

"There is no connection between the Church and matters of business in the home," he said. "Were we ever told that we cannot maintain discipline among our slaves?"

"Is this the teaching of Christ, or the philosophy of Mithra?" Apphia demanded.

"He has broken the law, and under the law he must be punished," Philemon continued as though he had not heard. "Where would we stand in our community if we did not kill this man? How would we be looked upon by those who also have slaves to keep in order? What would they say of our *mercy* as an example to the slaves of Colossae?"

"The law of the Romans reads that you *can* punish a slave," Apphia protested further. "It does not read that you *must*. The law of God demands mercy!"

"This man has not told us what we ought to know," Archippus added. "Is he possessed by an evil spirit? Is someone tempting us? Father, listen to me, for I am uneasy."

"What master am I," Philemon exclaimed, "that I cannot do what I would in my own house?"

"He need not have come back," Apphia said softly.

"That is what I do not understand," Archippus said again.

I did my best to raise myself on one arm. "Master," I gasped, "I am sorry for what . . . in my youthful . . . blindness. . . ."

Philemon looked at me long. I must have been a fearful sight, bleeding and bruised, quite unable to lift myself from the floor. Apphia stood by, silently now, while Archippus waited.

Suddenly Philemon shouted, "Zalgrebbo, leave the room!"

Zalgrebbo left, walking backwards in obvious amazement. I heard other sounds, whispers from the hall. The servants must have been watching. After a moment there was silence.

My master returned to his writing desk and sat down heavily.

"He was Persilio's playmate," he said as if talking to himself. "But for me to grant forgiveness in my heart, I cannot find that possible."

He put his head in his hands.

"My husband," Apphia said, "in time you will see his goodness again."

The moment had come. To delay speaking longer

would be but false vanity and wilful pride that would harm the purpose of Paul's message to Colossae.

I rose to my feet and took a stumbling step toward Philemon.

"Master, still I ask forgiveness from your heart, now," I said. "I have become a Christian."

Philemon looked up very slowly. Archippus stirred. Apphia drew a quick breath.

"What do you mean?" Philemon demanded.

"That I will redeem myself to you in any way that you wish, as I may now hope that I have been redeemed before Jesus Christ."

A long, long silence followed.

"You have become a Christian?" Archippus asked.

"Yes."

"Why did you not say so?"

"You know that I could not—until now."

The silence grew longer, until Philemon finally broke it.

"Who am I to withhold pardon? I have been made to see what I did not see. You are forgiven, my son—from my heart."

It is difficult for me to write of what happened then. I know that I became as a small boy. I fell to my knees before Philemon with tears of contrition, and all the dreadful events of the days and years seemed to be released from my soul.

Archippus stood by, not yet entirely satisfied. When I was able to stand again shamefaced, he asked further things.

"You were baptized in Rome? By whom?"

"By Paul of Tarsus, apostle of Christ."

"Paul!" Philemon said.

"I traveled here with Tychicus, sent by Paul with a letter to the church of Colossae." I hesitated a moment. "Master, Paul has sent to you a letter, in my care."

I withdrew the packet from my tunic. My master took it, and slowly broke open the seal.

"May God forgive me," he said in a low voice. He laid open the letter, while Apphia and Archippus stood by. I moved back from their circle.

My master read:

Paul, a prisoner for Christ Jesus, and Timothy our brother,

To Philemon our beloved fellow worker and Apphia our sister and Archippus our fellow soldier, and the church in your house:

Grace to you and peace from God our Father and the Lord Jesus Christ.

I thank my God always when I remember you in my prayers, because I hear of your love and of the faith which you have toward the Lord Jesus and all the saints, and I pray that the sharing of your faith may promote the knowledge of all the good that is ours in Christ. For I have derived much joy and comfort from your love, my brother, because the hearts of the saints have been refreshed through you.

Accordingly, though I am bold enough in Christ to command you to do what is required, yet for love's sake I prefer to appeal to you—I, Paul, an ambassador and now a prisoner also for Christ Jesus—I appeal to you for my child, Onesimus, whose father I have become in my imprisonment. (Formerly he was useless to you, but now he is indeed useful to you and to me.) I am sending him back to you, sending my very heart. I would have been glad to keep him with me, in order that he might serve me on your behalf during my imprisonment for the gospel; but I preferred to do nothing without your consent in order that your good-

*ness might not be by compulsion but of your own
free will.*

*Perhaps this is why he was parted from you for
a while, that you might have him back for ever, no
longer as a slave but more than a slave, as a beloved brother, especially to me but how much
more to you, both in the flesh and in the Lord. So
if you consider me your partner, receive him as
you would receive me.*

*If he has wronged you at all, or owes you any-
thing, charge that to my account. I, Paul, write this
with my own hand, I will repay it—to say nothing
of your owing me even your own self. Yes, brother, I want some benefit from you in the Lord. Re-
fresh my heart in Christ.*

*Confident of your obedience, I write to you,
knowing that you will do even more than I say. At
the same time, prepare a guest room for me, for I
am hoping through your prayers to be granted to
you.*

*Epaphras, my fellow prisoner in Christ Jesus,
sends greeting to you, and so do Mark, Aristarchus, Demas, and Luke, my fellow workers.*

*The grace of the Lord Jesus Christ be with your
spirit.*

When he had finished, Philemon rose to his feet and
walked over to one of the windows of his room. Already
Archippus had moved away, head bowed low, his back
to the rest of us.

Apphia sat on a couch. She was crying.

My own tumult of feeling cannot be described. That
Paul would go so far concerning me—Onesimus, the
one not useful but proven worthless—was beyond my
understanding.

I found my voice. "Master," I said, "I wish to return
to Paul in Rome."

"I understand," Philemon said. "He could have commanded me in all these things, but he did not. He has left all in my hands."

After a pause he said, "I have gained a son again, only to lose him so soon."

"I will come back, master," I said. "This is my home."

Philemon linked his hands and bowed his head. He said in prayer, "Christ our Lord, forgive us for these sins which in blindness we have committed even in your name, and grant that we may live hereafter in one mind with the Spirit."

XXI

As soon as it could be done, Philemon not only granted me freedom from slavery, but acquired for me the name and rights of a citizen of the Roman Empire.

Citizenship for one under thirty years was most unusual, as the Lex Junia, the Roman law governing manumission, provided that slaves under thirty years of age could be freed only as "latins," the name for a state of existence between slavery and freedom. None but a council of twenty Roman citizens, acting for justifiable cause, could make exception.

Philemon requested the council of Colossae to meet in extraordinary session to grant to his slave full freedom and citizenship. It was a mark of the highest respect to Philemon that they did so, despite the fact that by now everyone of the city knew me to be a returned fugitive. Few of the council were Christians, but as a body they honored Philemon's request.

Some time had to pass before these acts were completed. Meanwhile, Tychicus, now a guest of Philemon's household, delivered Paul's letter to the Colossian church. It was read to the congregation at services in the villa of Philemon, and so also was the letter from Paul concerning me.

The effect on the Christians of Colossae was immediate and remarkable. They had indeed been given over to quarreling and bitterness among themselves, to dissension and disturbance within their own families, to licentiousness in entertainment and sharp practices in business. They had reverted to beliefs in mystical beings and spirits inhabiting the earth and air. They had forsaken all except the name alone of Christ, and even his name had become a hollow shell.

Paul's words, with the explanations of Tychicus, came upon them like fresh air, bringing great revelations. They put away false ideals, for basically they were people sincere at heart in their desire to worship God.

I may say that in these things I found myself taking a small part. More than once I preached to the congregation, making use of what I knew from Paul's dictations. I talked with some men and women in their homes, and took special care to associate with the slaves of various households that I might carry to them the assurance of redemption.

In all these matters astonishing results were achieved among the Colossians.

Of special interest to me was the change wrought upon Archippus. He retired into his cell with the letter of Paul, and spent two days in study. Then he summoned me.

"Onesimus," he said, "at one time I blamed your crimes against Mithra for the death of Persilio. I know now, of course, how wrong I was."

"At one time I also blamed myself," I replied.

"I remember the girl who was sacrificed on the altar of the grotto," he said. "That appeasement of the god was wrong."

"Light of understanding comes slowly," I said. "It has ever been so."

"I believed that I took to privation and starvation in order to contemplate Christ," he said. "Instead, I was taking pride in a self-imposed misery. I was wrong, for in his letter Paul says: 'Why do you submit to regulations, *Do not handle, Do not taste, Do not touch* (referring to things which all perish as they are used), according to human precepts and doctrines? These have indeed an appearance of wisdom in promoting rigor of devotion and self-abasement and severity to the body, but they are of no value in checking the indulgence of the flesh.' "

"Yes," I said. Then I added Paul's following words, which I remembered: " 'If then you have been raised with Christ, seek the things that are above, where Christ is, seated at the right hand of God. Set your minds on things that are above, not on things that are on earth.' "

"And I was wrong also in leading others of Colossae into an abandonment of the world," Archippus said, "urging them to fast and to seek visions in solitude. For Paul writes to those others, 'Let no one disqualify you, insisting on self-abasement and worship of angels, taking his stand on visions, puffed up without reason by his sensuous mind, and not holding fast to the Head, from whom the whole body, nourished and knit together through its joints and ligaments, grows with a growth that is from God.' "

"That is how Paul wrote, by his own words," I told him. "You have read what he addressed to you in person, 'See that you fulfill the ministry which you have received in the Lord.' "

"Tell Paul, when you see him," Archippus said, "that I have taken heed."

From that time Archippus put away his solitude, and sought the company of men and women that he might spread among them the gospel of Christ. And other men followed him, and he became the leader of them in the ministry of the Lord.

When the day came for me to leave Colossae, I said a long farewell to all. Apphia and Philemon embraced me. So did Archippus, and Tychicus whom I would miss on the return journey. I had redeemed myself in the sight of men, and hoped to do the same in the eyes of God. It was difficult to make my departure, but I knew that I was more strongly called to Rome, to finish that which had been left undone.

The one who had been my master, Philemon, gave me of his worldly wealth sufficient for my journey, and more. I carried messages from them all to Paul.

So I set forth to Ephesus, on the first stage of my journey, astride the best horse and in company of three soldiers whom Philemon insisted on sending for my safety. Yet I rode in humility of spirit, for I think that pride of self can never be a part of me again.

My journey was long and filled with delays. Winter came, so that ships were held in ports by adverse weather. My impatience availed nothing. By necessity I had to bide my time, and before I saw once more the green shores and gray mountains of Italy, the season had turned to summer.

Again I landed at Puteoli, far to the south of Rome; but within the first two hours of being on land, I heard fearful news there which filled me with foreboding.

I had taken a place at an inn to rest, and then gone to the public room to dine. Other travelers were there, and by chance I overheard a conversation between two of them.

"I hear that they carried her head to Poppaea, the

Emperor's wife," one was saying to the other. "Nero has decreed public celebrations for his deliverance."

"To celebrate his infamy," the other said.

"Shh—who listens? Who knows what trouble is abroad?"

I knew not of whom they spoke, but having heard this much, I asked in curiosity: "Whose head? And is *Poppaea* the wife of the Emperor?" Noticing the astonishment of the two men, I added quickly, "Pardon me, I am just in from the sea."

They hesitated. "I can believe you," one said. "One should not speak too freely now. So you have not heard? Octavia has been killed at Pandateria by order of Caesar."

"Or the order of Poppaea!" the other said more outspokenly. "It was a ghastly deed."

"Octavia!" I cried. "But she was the wife of Nero!"

"Not after the divorce. You *are* behind the news, friend." He went on to tell me that Nero had divorced Octavia and had immediately married Poppaea. But the people of Rome were not satisfied by this dismissal of their favorite. Nero had found himself in serious trouble with the populace, until he was able to justify himself by charging Octavia with adultery with Anicetus, Prefect of the Imperial Fleet and murderer of Agrippina, Caesar's mother.

The traveler shrugged his shoulders. "Who knows the truth? Several of her servants testified to her infidelity."

I felt that the room was closing in over my head. "Her servants?"

"They testified under torture, of course. You know that the law allows slaves to testify against their own masters in cases of adultery. I suppose that by the method of torture one might confess anything." He misunderstood my horrified expression. "Oh, not all of them so testified. The story in Rome is that the others denied

Octavia's guilt. Nero needed only one or two confessions to prove his case."

I leaned toward him. "What then?"

Both men became suspicious.

"Hold, friend! One might think that it did mean something to you, after all."

"The rest of the story is as we told you," the other said. "Octavia was banished to the island of Pandateria —off the coast above here, you know. There it seems that she plotted with Anicetus to seize the fleet and overthrow Caesar. It became necessary that she be put to death as a traitor."

"And as I told you in the beginning, her head was carried up to Rome for Poppaea to see," the first man said.

"What of the slaves?"

"Slaves? How should we know?"

"Thank you," I said.

I had heard enough. Stunned, I moved away from them.

Aurelia—Aurelia, my beloved! What disaster had befallen?

All thought of dining left my mind. I went to the keeper of the inn, and with the resources now at my command I hired a chariot and driver to take me at the greatest possible speed to Rome.

In a brief time I was racing up the road to the north as fast as the two horses and driver could take me. Although the wheels thundered over the dusty highway and cobbled paving, and those along the route made haste to clear the way, yet in my anxiety we seemed to move as a snail.

What I might do in Rome, I could not even guess.

By necessity we paused at nightfall, but at the first light of day we were off again. Twice we found changes of horses. Then at last we drove from the Alban hills down the Appian Road into the valley of the Tiber.

By the time we passed through the gate of Rome, twilight had come once more.

I kept my driver as far as the Via Lata. I could ride openly through the city streets now, standing in the chariot as we passed the Circus Maximus and under the vast palaces of the Palatine. There I dismissed the chariot before reaching the house of Paul.

The last short distance I completed on foot. I found the house dark and shuttered. No guard stood in front, and the place was deserted.

My foreboding grew a hundredfold. What had happened to the apostle and all in his household? I had returned to a tragic Rome. My imagination conjured up all the worst things—not too extreme for the truth, as I came to learn.

For a moment I was at a loss—not knowing where to go. The city seemed ominous and evil. I thought of Calpurnius Rufus, the Christian with the mansion on the Quirinal hill.

Here was hope, but I hurried there through the dark streets with a mind filled by panic. I reached the locked gate, and knocked loudly to rouse a servant. For a long time I received no answer, but I persisted out of desperation.

A light appeared at last, and a voice called through the gate, "Who is it that knocks at this hour?"

"I wish to see Calpurnius Rufus," I replied. "It is most urgent."

"Who are you?" the servant demanded.

"I am Onesimus of Colossae, just now arrived in Rome. I must see Calpurnius."

"For what purpose at this hour of night? Give a reason, that we may know this is no trick of thieves."

"Open then to a Christian."

"That is enough."

The bars were withdrawn. The gate swung open, and

I entered into the garden. The air was sweet there with flowers in the hot night. Then the servant secured the locks again, and led me by torchlight to the house.

Calpurnius received me at once, although of course he had no remembrance of me. Quickly I was able to assure him of my identity, and that I had once been of Paul's household.

"You know nothing then?" he asked. "The news I must tell you is sad. Paul was taken alone before Caesar for judgment. He is now in the dungeon of the Mamertine Prison."

"Paul—in prison!"

"I cannot tell you the sentence, but I fear the worst."

"Where are the others? Timothy, Epaphras. . . ."

"Some of them had gone on travels before this happened. Timothy, for one, was sent off on business by Paul. Epaphras is in Rome. Demas has deserted in this hour of trouble."

Demas I had not known well.

"And . . . there was a girl named Florentina, of your congregation?"

His face remained grave as he shook his head. "I do not know," he said. "She must have been among those tortured by Nero to admit the infidelity of their mistress. It is known that several refused to comply, and are supposed to have paid an even greater penalty. I have heard no more."

"Where can I find Epaphras?"

"Not tonight. You will stay here and I can tell you how to find him in the morning. Remember, there is grave danger now for all who were with Paul."

"I would like to seek him tonight."

"Impossible! You will find him tomorrow in the Suburra through a woman who sells oil and fruits at a certain stall of the market there. I will tell you exactly where to go."

Nothing more could be done until daylight. I paced the floor of my room, sleepless that night.

In the morning I found the market stall in the Suburra district of Rome, as Calpurnius had directed. An elderly woman behind the counter sold olive oil, ripe peaches, and strawberries. I went straightaway to her and began to examine the strawberries.

"These appear good," I said. I made sure that no ear to hear was close. "I seek Epaphras, formerly of Colossae, now of Rome. Where may I find him?"

"The strawberries are fresh picked this morning," the woman said, picking up a few. "The best in the city, and low in price."

She was studying me.

"Who wants to know this thing?" she asked.

"Onesimus, also of Colossae, and just returned from there. He knows well."

A customer came to the counter.

"If you do not like these berries then," the fruit woman scolded, "return in one hour and I will have even more. You are a particular one, I have to say!"

"Are you certain that it will take an hour?" I asked her. "I am very impatient about these berries."

"I told you an hour!" she snapped. "I cannot do the impossible."

I bowed. "You will do me a special favor by making certain that they are good."

I left the stall, and walked off through the streets. The day was hot, and the sunlight shimmered along the pavement and from the brick housefronts. Remembering earlier lessons, I walked with apparent purpose to avoid undue curiosity. I made my way past the palace of Nero and through the Forum, a place where I had not dared to venture since that day of my first arrival so long ago.

Rome was as vast, as confusing, and as busy as I had known it before. The streets were as filled, and the shops as laden with goods. I noticed again the many temples where people came and went through the porticos, and wondered how long the false gods could withstand the growing strength of the Christian faith. I saw citizens in togas, women in litters, and young men who went together in twos and threes. But this capital of the Empire had for me a different quality now—a sinister core formed of blood and death.

Beyond the Forum was the Mamertine Prison, dread place where the conquering heroes of Rome had for so long deposited their captives to be strangled. Paul was there, close behind those walls, but at this moment as far beyond my reach as if I had been still in Phrygia.

And was Aurelia somewhere in this massed assemblage of buildings and streets and people? Had she been left in Rome, or sent into exile with her mistress? Was she alive? My anxiety was like a burning fever.

I restrained myself, and did not return to the market stall until exactly at the hour. I found a customer already there, inspecting one of the peaches. I walked up and stood beside him, trying to catch the eye of the market woman.

"It is ripe for eating," I heard the customer say.

The voice of Epaphras!

He looked at me and laughed.

"You see, she has good fruit," he said. He turned to the woman. "I will take it."

He laid a coin on the counter. I was about to walk off with Epaphras, when the woman called me back.

"Your berries," she said. "You might well have forgotten them."

"Oh, yes." I reached for a coin.

"You *are* forgetful," she said. "You have already paid for them."

"Did I?" I took the basket of fruit she handed to me.

"My greatest thanks. I trust that you will find your reward in many ways."

"And you," she said.

As if we had been together all the while, Epaphras and I walked on together. He talked casually, and suggested that we have a cup of wine in a shop close at hand.

We found a darkened corner at the rear of the place. There Epaphras dropped his mask of casualness.

"My friend, I am so glad that you have come!" He kept his voice low. "I thought that it would never be. Yet you are almost too late."

"Paul?"

"In prison, as you may have heard. I fear to say it—the last hour is not far away."

"They—will put him to death?"

"Unless a miracle occurs, and I know not what such a miracle could be. Yet he wants it this way. He is strong, and he accepts it as God's will for him. I see him every day."

"May I, then?"

"I do not know. Perhaps. He has converted and baptized the very soldiers who guard him! It may be that they will allow you to come."

"Beg them—I have so many messages for him, and so much to say for myself!"

"I will try. Onesimus, I fear there is much news for you."

"A girl by name of Aurelia. . . . ?"

He nodded. By his expression I knew that something terrible had happened.

"I must tell you first that Aurelia became a Christian."

"Aurelia!"

"Yes. When she learned what you had done, she came to Paul and was baptized. Then. . . ."

"What?"

"You have heard the story of Octavia?"

"Yes. Quickly, tell me of Aurelia!"

"She and the others—Florentina, too—were put under torture to incriminate their mistress." He ran his hand over his face. "They would not. . . . I do not know how they kept themselves from it. . . ."

"Some did."

"Those were others, not Octavia's own serving girls. The ones who loved their mistress refused. One older woman of Octavia spat in the face of her torturer, so they say in the city."

"Where is Aurelia?"

"The State took the girls from Octavia, and sold them again. Florentina—thank God!—with help we could give at the right moment, was bought by a Christian family."

"And Aurelia?"

"She was sold to a house of prostitution."

I felt the shudder down my back.

"Where is it?"

"Wait, Onesimus, you can do nothing."

"I can see her."

Epaphras looked at me for a moment. "Very well," he said. "Listen to me . . . you have to know. Aurelia is . . . different. She has been under torture."

"You have seen her?"

"After she was sold, but before she was delivered to her new owner. We tried to stop it and could not."

I felt sick. But I rose unsteadily to my feet.

"Give me that address," I demanded.

He named a street on the northern edge of Rome, near the Tiber. "Ask there for the house of Chrysalia. It is well known in the neighborhood."

"I go at once," I said. "Where do I find you again?"

"Here in this shop, tomorrow at the same hour—if God wills it."

I started out, and discovered that I was still holding

the basket of strawberries. I carried them back.

"I cannot use these," I said to Epaphras. "Keep them."

XXII

The house of Chrysalia was small and shabby, on a poor street of the city.

My fear reached an almost unbearable point as I knocked on the door.

The answer was immediate, but the door opened only slightly.

"This is the place that belongs to Chrysalia?" I asked through the crack. "You have been well recommended to me."

"By whom?"

"One of your friends."

The door opened wider.

"You are early in the day," the woman inside said. "It is less than noon."

I laughed. "I am anxious," I told her.

"Very well, then," she said. She swung the door open. "Enter."

The woman was old. The interior of the house was dark, and perfume hung heavily in the air.

"I was told that you had a girl by name of Aurelia," I said. "She is the one for me."

"Aurelia?" she asked in astonishment. "Who would speak to you of her? You would not care for that one. She is crippled."

"That is the one," I said. "That describes her. Aurelia, or no one!"

The old woman shrugged her shoulders. "There is always something new," she said. "Still—this way."

She led me to the back of the house. All was very quiet.

"Aurelia can play music," she called back. "You would like that, perhaps?"

"Yes, that would be nice," I said.

"Wait here."

The woman disappeared into a room, and I heard low voices. The time that passed seemed forever.

Suddenly the soft notes of a lyre reached me, and I heard a sweet song in Aurelia's voice . . . but so melancholy.

The old woman returned. She nodded. "Enter," she said. "I warned you. If you want to change to another, I will arrange it."

"My thanks," I said humbly.

I walked into the room.

It was dark except for a small lamp hidden behind a screen. No window admitted daylight, and I could make out no more than a dim form in white on the edge of a couch.

She could not see my face in the shadows.

"May we have more light?" I asked.

The music stopped abruptly. Did my voice awaken something?

After a moment she said, "It is better this way."

I walked to the screen around the lamp and removed it. Light flowed across the room. I turned quickly to face her.

She gave a startled cry.

I ran to her, with my arms held out. "Aurelia! At last!"

But she shook her head and turned away. "No, no, no, no! Why have you come here?"

I took her face between my hands. I turned her head

so that she looked at me. The light from the lamp shone full on her.

A red scar crossed the length of her cheek, from ear to chin.

"Onesimus!" she murmured incredulously. "So this is why someone asked for me."

"They did not touch your eyes," I said. "Like dark blue pools that reach so deep."

"Onesimus, I am lame! They pulled my legs so that I cannot walk straight any more."

"It does not matter."

"Why did you come to me? Why did you not go to one of the other girls?"

"Aurelia!"

"Go, please. I wish that you had stayed away."

"Aurelia, my love, listen to me."

"If this is not enough, then look! *Look!*"

She swung around on the couch, at the same time letting the gown around her shoulders fall. I saw her naked back, and across it the angry lines of a multitude of scars—scars from burning irons.

"Now, do you still want me? You will prefer another, in the next room. . . ."

I clutched her hands. "I want you, forever," I said. "Scars will fade and in faith you will walk firmly with me. The miracle has come to pass. . . ."

When I went to tell the woman Chrysalia that I wished to purchase Aurelia from her, I ran into opposition.

"I have too few here as it is," she said.

"You told me that she was crippled and of little use."

"She plays music," the old woman said. "She has value."

"I will pay," I said.

She frowned. "Why do you want her? There must be some reason."

"Would you make the Emperor himself come here to take her?" I said sharply. "You know what price you would receive then."

It was a gamble on my part. Stories of Nero's licentiousness and the warped forms of his orgies had long been current.

"That is different," Chrysalia said hastily. "You may have her."

The business was done and the documents signed. Aurelia was made over to my ownership.

Then we went out into the open air, the bright sunlight of freedom. "I am dreaming," Aurelia said.

Yet she pulled her hood close against her face to hide the scar. And she limped with a jerking sideways motion, for one of her legs was twisted.

I took her to the office of the magistrate, and there he performed the formalities of granting Aurelia freedom. Under the law governing age, it had to be done in the status of "latin," not yet in citizenship rank. It mattered very little.

For on that same afternoon Aurelia and I were married in the full sense of the Roman law.

XXIII

Epaphras arranged that on the following night in the darkest hour we were to visit Paul in prison.

The three of us went together through the streets, and cautiously approached the gates of the Mamertine Prison.

"Who comes?" the first guard demanded. He raised a torch high to see.

"You know me," Epaphras said. "Listen: The Cross is for redemption."

"Pass," the guard whispered, and he lowered the torch.

At the gate two more guards also let us pass. Here Epaphras paused.

"Continue," he said to Aurelia and to me. "This night I will wait here."

We went on. I held Aurelia's hand as she limped at my side. The men of the Praetorian Guard were expecting us. They nodded, without speaking. At the sight of the short swords and soldiers' regalia Aurelia held back, but I reassured her.

We were in a room of gray stone walls, where sputtering torches smoked in their holders. One guard pulled away planks from over a hole in the stone floor. Another brought a wooden ladder and tilted it down into the cavern below.

"Descend," one whispered. "And make sure that you stay but briefly. If this should be discovered. . . ."

"Onesimus!" Aurelia said. "I cannot."

She shrank back from the hole in the floor.

"Aurelia, yes."

"It is my leg," she whispered. "I cannot descend by that ladder."

"You can, of course. Paul awaits." I led her to the edge of the cavern. "I will go first. You follow close to me."

I placed my feet on the rungs and began to descend. Then, with a helping hand from a soldier, Aurelia did the same. Her crippled leg made it exceedingly difficult; yet slowly we moved down into the darkness.

At one point Aurelia uttered a slight cry of pain. I thought that she might fall, and I held up my hand to steady her.

At length my foot touched the dungeon floor. A lamp burned with a tiny flame against a wall, doing little to dispel the darkness. The air was close, smelling of human bodies and stale blood.

I heard a chain rattle in the darkness. When Aurelia reached my side, we turned to see the silent figure of Paul himself standing before us. His face shone with welcoming joy.

He held out his arms and embraced each of us. "My son! My daughter!"

"Master," I replied in a voice choked with feeling.

"I am happy that you have come," he said. "As God has brought you both together, so He has led you to me. What is the news from Colossae?"

I told Paul all that had occurred there. He nodded with satisfaction. "And Tychicus stays?" he asked.

"Yes, master. He has been in Colossae and at Laodicea. Later he moves on to Ephesus."

Also I gave to Paul the special message from Archippus. He nodded again.

"Now I will speak," he said. "There is no more for you to do in Rome. I would that you leave at once, both of you—*at once,* I say, before it comes to be too late. At once—tonight or tomorrow! Do not delay for the trip to Puteoli, but go by way of Ostia."

"Why, master, what will happen here?"

"Listen to what I say. Go! Return to Asia, and to the cities there. That is your home, and there you will be most needed—Onesimus, the useful one."

"Yes, master."

"Make certain of this Church of God against all enemies. For now I believe that the Church will continue as the living evidence of the word of God. Pass along what I say to all whom you see, in spite of everything."

"I will, master."

"My son and my daughter, you have gained faith by the hard road. Let it never be shaken."

"Master, never."

A soldier leaned over the opening of light above. "Haste," he called down. "It is time."

"Oh, my master . . . !"

I could check myself no longer. I fell to my knees before him—and Aurelia did, too.

"My strength is in the Lord," Paul said. "Do not fear for me, I rejoice that the hour comes. Do you rejoice likewise, my children. Depart now."

Paul placed his hands on our heads. "The peace of God, which passes all understanding, shall keep your hearts and minds through Jesus Christ. God will bless you, Onesimus and Aurelia. We are to meet again in the kingdom of God."

He lifted us to our feet. I heard the sound of the chain by which he was bound. I clasped one hand, and Aurelia took another.

"Master," she whispered, "we thank our God for you."

Paul for the space of one breath trembled. *We thank our God for you.* Such simple words from one heart gave expression to the reward on earth for Paul of Tarsus.

The soldier called again, and we left Paul standing there. How we stumbled up that ladder from the dungeon with our eyes so blinded by tears I know not. The guards reached down to help us to the upper floor, and hastily they led us to the gate.

Epaphras joined us. We could not speak for our grief, not until we were gone from the prison and out into the streets of Rome. We walked quickly, not knowing the direction or purpose, past the silent temples and the palaces and shrines of the city.

Suddenly Aurelia stopped. She stared at me. By the starlight of the summer night, I saw her eyes widen and widen.

"Onesimus! I am walking straight!"

I had not thought of it. But, yes, she had walked all this way without a limp!

"Going down the ladder," she said, "I must have stretched my leg that time. . . ." She stopped.

From the hair on my head, down my spine and to my toes I felt the prickling of my flesh.

"No!" Aurelia said. Her hand went to her mouth. "Paul. . . ."

Calpurnius Rufus took care of us in his house that night, and on the following day we hurried by horseback to the port of Ostia at the mouth of the Tiber. Aurelia rode with me, and a man came with us as escort. Who he was, or to whom the horses belonged, we did not know. Epaphras in Rome bade us farewell, and he instructed us to ask no questions. A ship sailing for Greece held its departure until our arrival. Arrangements for our passages had already been completed. To such extent has grown the Christian congregation of Rome.

We sailed at once, and cleared the breakwater of Ostia in far different circumstances than on my last doomed departure there. Aurelia and I clasped hands as we stood on deck to watch the fading shore. Our hearts and minds were too full to speak.

With these words I bring to an end this account of a search for faith. Each man seeks for himself, by one way or another, until he finds it.

Even as I finish this writing, our ship approaches the shore of Athens, and around us lie the islands of Greece on the sunny sea. Now I, Onesimus, and Aurelia, my dearly beloved, salute each one of you. The grace of God be with you always.